Dotnetuncle's Interview Crackerjack

By Vishal K. Khanna

My family is my source of energy. I dedicate this book to them. That includes my daughter Elena, my wife Mandeep, Mom and Dad.

- Vishal K. Khanna

Preface

I had a habit of exploring new technical platforms, primarily driven around the Microsoft basket. This habit drove me to explore new dimensions in the galactic space of technologies, industries, management practices and business verticals. To ensure I was successful at what I was doing, I had to study and practice a lot, and stay glued at work. During my practice sessions, I had a habit of jotting a lot of notes. One day, sometime in the year 2005, I realized that there was quite limited interview preparation material available on the web, and there are many people around who need ready-to-eat study material for preparing for their interviews. That's when I thought of creating a website and publish my notes.

In the beginning, I used Googlepages, and later I created Dotnetuncle.com. This website gradually grew and turned out to be a sizable repository of Interview FAQs with answers. A lot of people started writing to me with good and bad feedback. I kept on trying to consistently improve the website. The years 2008-2009 witnessed a lot of changes in the website. Today the website draws a lot of self perpetuated web traffic due its popularity. People still write to me. Many of the website visitors requested me to write a book on .NET interview questions. It's always tough get into a self-motivated project, but then, writing is my passion.

So I thought let me give it a go, and here comes "Dotnetuncle's Interview Crackerjack". This book is my first book, and I've triggered all bazookas to pump in a wide array of questions-answers with this pack. The questions are derived from my programming experience, giving & taking interviews, answering questions on technical forums, scrutinizing frequently asked questions and compiling them. It is also a bag of interview questions asked by colossal IT companies.

There are many refinements and additions in this book, as to what is there in my website, and there is a huge chunk of new interview questions. That includes topics such as .NET 4.0, MVC and Silverlight.

A few words for the readers of this book: If you are giving a technical interview, you are facing a tough job. But also remember that the interviewer has a tougher job because he/she has hardly any time to judge you and pick the best fit. The interviewer's questions might range from Arctic to Antarctica. But don't worry, keep on reading and life will be cruising. I've tried to formulate this book in such a way that it covers the easy and tough questions from a broad variety of topics. One fact always remains that most of us never know how technically strong the interviewer is. Nevertheless, you cannot fluke around, and rather be rock solid prepared. May this material be useful to you, and I wish you all the best!

Each question in this book has been assigned a difficulty level, defined as follows:

★ Beginner Level

★★ Intermediate Level

★★★ Advanced Level

Before summing up, I would like to thank all those who wanted me to write this book. Big thanks to my mom (Indu Khanna) who taught me so many good things in life, my dad (Arun Khanna) who always wanted me to be successful, my grandpa (Late J.N.Khanna) who taught me a lot of discipline, and all my gurus in college, office and technical forums. Lastly, a super-special thanks to my wife (Mandeep Khanna) who regularly motivates me to keep on doing something cool, and my lovely little daughter Elena who always wants me to play games, and do nothing other than that. Above all, thank you God.

TABLE OF CONTENTS

CHAPTER 1 – Object Oriented Programming System

Q1. ★What is OOPS?
A1. No doubt, everything in the world can be perceived as an object. The type of the object may vary. A bottle of wine is an object. If the bottle of wine is to be treated as some kind of entity in the programming world, it is treated as an object. In OOPS, we get the power to create objects of our own, as & when required. OOPS is a programming methodology where each entity is an object. You may create your own wine, cheers!

It is a method of computer programming where entities of related data together with routines associated with it are treated as one object in the program. The programming techniques can include programming concepts such as **polymorphism, inheritance, data abstraction and encapsulation.**

Objects started being used in the world of computers during the 1950's in the LISP programming language *(which is a language in use even today for apps on artificial intelligence)*. LISP has items called as **atom** which have attributes associated to them. The concept of Objects, Classes and Instances was formally introduced during the 1960's in a programming language called Simula 67. Down the line, the concept of Object Oriented Programming was introduced in Smalltalk by Smalltalk PARC. OOPS gradually kept on evolving with maturity. Later C++ was launched with a wide array of OOPS features.

Languages on the .NET Framework such as C#.NET and VB.NET are based on OOPS.

Q2. ★What is a Class? What is a Base Class?
A2. A class is an organized store-house in object-oriented programming that gives coherent functional abilities to a group of related code. It is the definition of an object. Using classes, we may wrap data and behavior together (that's called **Encapsulation**). We may define classes in terms of classes (that's called **Inheritance**). We can also override the behavior of a class using an alternate behavior (that's called **Polymorphism**).

It is important to note that a class is a **Reference Type**. A class of reference type basically means that its instances are processed on heap in the memory by the .NET runtime engine *(i.e. the CLR)*.

A **Base Class** is a class that is inherited by another class.

> **Important**: In .NET, a class may inherit from only one class.

Q3. ★What is Encapsulation?
A3. Encapsulation is the ability of an object to hide its data and methods from the rest of the world. It is one of the fundamental principles of OOPS.

Say we create a class named Calculations. This class may contain a few members in the form of properties, events, fields or methods. Once the class is created, we may instantiate the class by creating an object out of it. The object acts as an instance of this class, the members of the class are not exposed to the outer world directly; rather, they are encapsulated by the class.

Example(C#):

```
Public class Calculations
{
  private void fnMultiply(int x, int y)
  {
    return x * y;
  }
}
...
...
Calculations obj;
int Result;
Result = obj.fnMultiply(5,10);
```

As demonstrated by the code above, the object of the class **Calculations** named **obj** doesn't expose the how its method **fnMultiply** is processing what is passed to it. So eventually all properties, functions etc. inside the class are said to be encapsulated as they contain everything. They can be used easily, and yet don't expose the intricacies to the outside world.

Q4. ★What is inheritance?
A4. Inheritance is the concept of passing the traits of a class to another class.

A class comprises of a collection of types of encapsulated instance variables and types of methods, events, properties, possibly with implementation of those types together with a constructor function that can be used to create objects of the class. A class is a cohesive package that comprises of a particular kind of compile-time metadata. A Class describes the rules by which objects behave; these objects are referred to as **instances** of that class.

Classes can inherit from another class. This is accomplished by **putting a colon** after the class name when declaring the class. Generally, these relationships are called **parent-child relationships** where the parent class is on the left side of the colon, and the child class is on the right side of the colon.

Example (C#):

```
Class parent:child
{
  .....
}
```

Q5. ★What is a class member? What is an object?
A5. The entities such as events, properties, fields and functions encapsulated within a class are called **class members**. A constructor of a class that resides within it is also a form of a class member.

When we instantiate a class in order to use its encapsulated class members, this instantiated class entity is called the **object**.

Q6. ★What is polymorphism? How to achieve polymorphism?

A6. **Polymorphism** means allowing a single function definition to be used with different types of data (specifically, different classes of objects). For example, a polymorphic function definition can replace several type-specific ones, and a single polymorphic operator can act in expressions of various types. Many programming languages implement some forms of polymorphism.

The concept of polymorphism applies to data types in addition to functions. A function that can evaluate to and be applied to values of different types is known as a **polymorphic function**. A data type that contains elements of different types is known as a **polymorphic data type**.

Polymorphism may be achieved by overloading a function, overloading an operator, changing the order of types, changing the types using the same name for the member in context.

Example(C#):

```
Public class Calc
{
   public void fnMultiply(int x, int y)
   {
    return x * y;
   }
   public void fnMultiply(int x, int y, int z)
   {
    return x * y * z; }
   }
   ...
   ...
   Calc obj;
   int Result;
   Result = obj.fnMultiply(2,3,4); // The second fnMultiply would be called
   Result = obj.fnMultiply(3,4); // The first fnMultiply would be called
```

Here, the call depends on the number of parameters passed. Polymorphism is achieved using overloading.

Q7. ★ What is a property? Explain the keyword 'value'.
A7. **Property** - A property is a programming entity that describes the features of an object. A property is a piece of data contained within a class that has an exposed interface for reading and writing. Looking at this definition, we might think we could declare a public variable in a class and call it a property. While this assumption is somewhat valid, the real technical term for a public variable in a class is a field. The main difference between a field and a property is in the inclusion of an interface.

We make use of **Get** and **Set** keywords while working with properties. We prefix the variables used within this code block with an underscore *(that's the preferred way)*. **Value** is a keyword that holds the value which is being retrieved or set.

Example (VB):

```
Private _Color As String
  Public Property Color()
  Get
     Return _Color
  End Get
  Set(ByVal Value)
     _Color = Value
  End Set
End Property
```

Q8. ★What is an event?

A8. **Event** - An event is an action that an object does. When something happens, we say an event has happened. For example, when a button is clicked, we say it is the click() event. When a mouse hovers on an image, we say the mouseover( ) event has taken place.

Q9. ★What is an access modifier?

A9. **Access Modifiers** – are keywords used to change the way members of a class are accessed. The main purpose of using access specifiers is to provide security to the code of the application. The availability *(scope)* of the member objects of a class may be controlled using access specifiers.

Q10. ★Explain the access specifiers Public, Private, Protected, Friend, Internal and Default.

A10. The different access specifiers are explained below:

PUBLIC - as the name signifies, the members under this access specifier's scope can be accessed from anywhere. If a member of a class is defined as public then it can be accessed anywhere in the class. It can also be accessed outside the class. This means that objects can access and modify public fields, properties, methods.

PRIVATE - as the name suggests, these members can't be accessed outside the class. It's the private property of the class and can be accessed only by the members of the class.

FRIEND/INTERNAL - Friend & Internal mean the same. Friend is used in VB.NET. Internal is used in C#. Friend members can be accessed by all classes within an assembly but not from outside the assembly.

PROTECTED - Protected variables can be used within the class as well as the classes that inherits this class.

PROTECTED FRIEND/PROTECTED INTERNAL - The Protected Friend can be accessed by members of the assembly or the inheriting class, and of course, within the class itself.

DEFAULT - A Default property is a single property of a class that can be set as the default. This allows developers that use your class to work more easily with your default property because they do not need to make a direct reference to the property.

> **Note**: Default properties cannot be initialized as Shared/Static or private, and all must be accepted at least on argument or parameter. Default properties do not promote good code readability, so use this option sparingly.

Q11. ★What is Overloading? What is Overloads? What is Overload?

A11. **Overloading** - is the concept of using one function or class in different ways by changing the signature of its parameters. We can define a function with multiple signatures without using the keyword **Overloads**, but if you use the Overloads keyword in one, you must use it in all of the function's Overloaded signatures.

The **Overloads** keyword is used in VB.NET; while the **Overload** keyword is used in C# (*There is no other difference*). The Overloads property allows a function to be described using different combinations of parameters. Each combination is considered a signature, thereby uniquely defining an instance of the method being defined.

> **Note:** Overloading is used to achieve polymorphism.

Q12. ★★What is the difference between Shared and Static?

A12. They both mean the same! Shared is used in VB.NET. Static is used in C#.

When the static keyword is used to declare a class, the member in context must be directly invoked from the class, rather than from the instance. Consider the following example

Example C#:

```
//Consider writing the following line of code...
Console obj = new Console();
obj.Writeline("I am drunk");  //This line doesn't print

//This doesn't work, because WriteLine is a static method defined in the class Console
//The Console class is a static class
```

To use static members, give a reference to the exact class, as an instance in this case won't work.

To make this work, write the following line of code:
```
Console.Writeline("I never get drunk"); // This line will print
```

> **Tip:** To work with members of static classes, there is no need to create their instances.

Q13. ★What is a Static Member?

A13. **Static Member** - The keyword static is used to create a static member. A static member is owned by the class, not by its instances (objects of the class).

Static members are actually class members *(members owned by the class)*, while non-static members) are instance members *(which means they are owned by the instances)*. In C# & VB.NET, we may create static/shared events, properties,   fields and functions.

> **Tip**: Indexers in C# cannot be declared static.
> **Note**: Static member functions cannot access non-static members directly.

Q14. ★★What are Indexers?
A14. An **indexer** is a medium in C-Sharp through which an index can be assigned to a class instance or a struct instance. That's somewhat similar to what an array does.

Q15. ★What is the virtual keyword used for? What is the base keyword?
A15. **Virtual** - If a base class method is to be overriden, it is defined using the keyword virtual (otherwise the **sealed** keyword is used to prevent overriding).

Note that the class member method may be overriden even if the virtual keyword is not used, but its usage makes the code more transparent & meaningful.

> **Note**: In VB.NET, we may use the **overridable** keyword for this purpose.

When the **override** keyword is used to override the virtual method, in a scenario where the base class method is required in a child class along with the overriden method, then the **base** keyword may be used to access the parent class member. The following code example will make the usage more clear.

Example(C#):

```
public class Employee
{
  public virtual void SetBasic(float money) //This method may be overriden
  {
    Basic += money;
  }
}

public class Manager : Employee
{
  public override void SetBasic(float money) //This method is being overriden
  {
    float managerIncentive = 10000;
    base.SetSalary(money + managerIncentive); //Calling base class method
  }
}
```

Q16. ★Explain overridable, overrides, notoverridable and mustoverride
A16. These keywords are used in VB.NET.

Overridable -The Overridable keyword is used when defining a property or method of an inherited class, as overridable by the inheriting class.

Overides - The Overides keyword allows the inheriting class to disregard the property or method of the inherited class and implements its own code.

NotOverridable - The NotOverridable keyword explicitly declares a property or method as not overridable by an inheriting class, and all properties are "not overridable" by default. The only real advantage of using this keyword is to make your code more readable.

MustOverride - The MustOverride keyword forces the inheriting class to implement its own code for the property or method.

Q17. ★What is shadowing? Explain the 'shadows' keyword?
A17. **Shadowing** - is a concept of altering the behavior of a base class member.

When you do shadowing, you provide a new implementation to the base class member without overriding it. You may shadow a base class member in a derived class, by using the keyword **shadows**. The access level, return type, and the signature *(i.e. the data types of the arguments passed & the order of the types)* of the derived class members which are shadowed, may differ from the base class.

In C#, you may achieve shadowing using the keyword **new**.

Q18. ★What is a constructor? Explain the 'new' Keyword.
A18. **Constructor** - A constructor is a function with the same name as that of the class. The Default Constructor of a class does not have an argument. The default constructor ensures that every data member is initialized to a default value. Constructors provide a way for classes to initialize a state for their members.

> **Note**: Constructors don't have a return type *(not even void)*.

Example (C#):

```
public SomeClass()
{
  Console.Writeline("Waiter says: Lets have one peg by default");
}

public SomeClass(string str)
{
  Console.Writeline("Waiter says: Lets have another peg along with " + str);
}
```

When a custom constructor is defined, the Default Constructor is not called. A constructor may also be overloaded.

New - This keyword may be used as a modifier and as an operator. When used as an operator, it creates an object on a heap to invoke constructors. When used as a modifier, it hides an inherited member from the base class member.

As an operator, it can be used to create an object and then to invoke the constructor of the class. See the example below:

Example (C#):

```
SomeClass objSomeClass = new SomeClass(); //Creating a class object and invoking its
constructor

float amount = new float(); //Creating an object of the type, and invoking its constructor
```

As a modifier, it is used to explicitly hide a member from the base class. See example:

Example (C#):

```
public class MamaClass
{
public void SomeMethod() { ... }
}

public class BabyClass : MamaClass
{
new public void SomeMethod() { .... }
}
```

Q19. ★★What is a Private Constructor?
A19. Private Constructor - When a constructor is created with a private specifier, it is neither possible for other classes to derive from this class, nor it is possible to create an instance of this class. They are usually used in classes that contain static members only. It is also used to create **Singleton** classes.

Q20. ★★What is a static constructor?
A20. Static Constructor - It is a special type of constructor, introduced with C#. It gets called before the creation of the first object of a class *(probably at the time of loading an assembly)*. See example below.

Example (C#):

```
public class SomeClass()
{
  static SomeClass()
  {
    //Static members may be accessed from here. Write the code for initialization
  }
}
```

Important: While creating a static constructor, a few things need to be kept in mind:
- ✓ There is no access modifier required to define a static constructor
- ✓ There may be only one static constructor in a class
- ✓ The static constructor may not have any parameters
- ✓ This constructor may only access the static members of the class
- ✓ We may create more than one static constructor for a class

Q21. ★Can a class be created without a constructor?
A21. No. In case we don't define the constructor, the class will access the no-argument constructor from its base class. The compiler will process this during compilation.

Q22. ★What is Serialization?
A22. **Serialization** – Serialization is the process of converting an object into a stream of bytes. This stream of bytes can be persisted. **Deserialization** is an opposite process, which involves converting a stream of bytes into an object. Serialization is used usually during remoting *(while transporting objects)* and to persist file objects & database objects.

.NET provides two ways for serialization:

- ✓ **XmlSerializer**
- ✓ **BinaryFormatter / SoapFormatter**

In general, the XmlSerializer is used for Web Services. The BinaryFormatter & SoapFormatter is used for Remoting. While using XmlSerializer, it is required that the target class has parameter less constructors, has public read-write properties and has fields that can be serialized. The XmlSerializer has good support for XML documents. It can be used to construct objects from existing XML documents. The XmlSerializer enables us to serialize and deserialize objects to an XML format.

SoapFormatter enables us to serialize & deserialize objects to SOAP format. They can serialize private and public fields of a class. The target class must be marked with the **Serializable** attribute.

Note: On deserialization, the constructor of the new object is not invoked.

The BinaryFormatter has the same features as the SoapFormatter except that it formats data into binary format. The BinaryFormatter *(and the SoapFormatter)* has two main methods - Serialize and Deserialize. To serialize an object, we pass an instance of the stream and the object to the Serialize method. To deserialize an object, you pass an instance of a stream to the Deserialize method. You can use the BinaryFormatter to serialize many, but not all classes in the .NET Framework. For example, you can serialize ArrayLists, DataSets, and Arrays but not other objects, such as DataReaders or TextBox controls.

Tip: To serialize a class, the class must have the Serializable attribute or implement the ISerializable interface.

Note that the XmlSerializer captures only the public members of the class, whereas the BinaryFormatter & the SoapFormatter captures both the public & private members of the class. The output using the BinaryFormatter is quite compact, as the information is in binary format, whereas the XmlSerializer format is filled with XML tags. See the example below:

Example (VB.NET):

```
Imports System.IO
Imports System.Runtime.Serialization.Formatters.Binary


Dim colArrayList As ArrayListDim
objFileStream As FileStreamDim
objBinaryFormatter As BinaryFormattercolArrayList = New ArrayList()
colArrayList.Add( "Jacobs Creek")
colArrayList.Add( "Smirnoff")
colArrayList.Add( "Bacardi White")
objFileStream = New FileStream(MapPath("C:\myArrayList.data"), FileMode.Create)
objBinaryFormatter = New BinaryFormatterobjBinaryFormatter.Serialize(objFileStream,
colArrayList)objFileStream.Close()
```

Here we see that an instance of the file stream *(objFileStream)* and an instance of the object *(colArrayList)* is passed to the Serialize method of the BinaryFormatter object *(objBinaryFormatter)*. We also end up creating a file by the name myArrayList.data on our hard-drive. In order to deserialize an object, see the code below:

```
Dim colArrayList As ArrayListDim objFileStream As FileStreamDim
objBinaryFormatter As BinaryFormatterDim strItem As String
objFileStream = New FileStream( MapPath("myArrayList.data"), FileMode.Open )
objBinaryFormatter = New BinaryFormatter
colArrayList = CType( objBinaryFormatter.Deserialize( objFileStream ), ArrayList )
objFileStream.Close()
For Each strItem In colArrayList
  Response.Write( " " & strItem )
Next
```

Here, CType takes in two parameters, the first parameter is the serialized object in the file stream format, and the second parameter is the desired type. Finally, the page iterates through all the elements of the ArrayList and displays the value of each element.

> **Note**: XmlSerializer does not serialize instances of classes such as Hashtable which implement the IDictionary interface.

Q23. ★What is the Serializable attribute used for?
A23. **Serializable** - This is a class attribute. When we use this attribute with a class, an instance of this class can be taken in whatever state it is, and write it to a disk *(memory)*. The class can then be deserialized, and the class will act as if it is simply stored in the memory.

Q24. ★What is a delegate?

A24. **Delegate** - It is a type safe function pointer. It is a type that holds the reference of a method. A delegate may be used to call a method asynchronously.

Q25. ★★What is a multicast delegate?
A25. **Multicast Delegate** - it is a delegate that holds reference of more than one method. Multicast Delegates must have a return type of void.

Q26. ★What is an abstract class?
A26. If a class is to serve the purpose of providing common fields and members to all subclasses, we create an Abstract class. For creating an abstract class, we make use of the abstract keyword. Such a class cannot be instantiated.

Q27. ★What is an interface? How to implement an interface?
A27. An **Interface** is a collection of semantically related abstract members. An interface expresses through the members it defines, the behaviors that a class needs to support. An interface is defined using the keyword interface. The members defined in an interface contain only definition, no implementation. The members of an interface are all public by default; any other access specifier cannot be used.

An interface is implemented using implements keyword. A class may implement more than one interface.

> **Note**: When a class inherits and implements at the same time, the inherited parent class name is written first, followed by the names of the interfaces to be implemented.

Q28. ★Is multiple inheritance possible in .NET?
A28. No. Multiple inheritance is not possible in .NET. This means it is not possible for one class to inherit from multiple classes. However, a class may implement multiple interfaces. We may also declare objects of different classes in a class. This way, the encapsulated class may be instantiated in other classes.

CHAPTER 2 – .NET Framework

Q1. ★Tell something about the Microsoft .NET Framework?
A1. **.NET** – is a software development framework by Microsoft Corporation. It is used to connect information, people, systems, and devices through software. Integrated across the Microsoft platform, .NET technology provides the ability to quickly build, deploy, manage, and use connected, security-enhanced solutions with Web services. .NET-connected solutions enable businesses to integrate their systems more rapidly and in a more agile manner. They help to realize the promise of information anytime, anywhere, on any device. It includes a massive library of functions and it supports many programming languages. The .NET Framework is mainly comprised of the .NET Libraries and the **Common Language Runtime** *(CLR)*, which is the runtime engine of .NET

Q2. ★Which languages can be used to program in .NET?
A2. Microsoft provides these languages for programming .NET - C#, VB.NET, JS.NET, C++.NET.

C++.NET may be used as a Managed Code Language by using managed extensions. This is done using a **_gc postfix**. A managed C++ class can inherit from VB.NET classes, C# classes, JS.NET classes. A managed class can inherit from only one class. .NET doesn't allow multiple inheritance in managed classes.

Any Language that has a compiler that can compile the language code to **MSIL** is a .NET compliant language. MSIL stands for Microsoft Intermediate Language.

Below is an alphabetical list of languages supported by .NET:

- ✓ **APL** - It is a language for describing procedures in the processing of information. It is a very powerful language. It may be used to describe mathematical procedures.
- ✓ **C++** - A widely known language. One of the oldest Object Oriented Languages, an advanced version of the C language. Microsoft has its own Visual C++ compiler that includes special tools and libraries for development on Windows platform. C++ is an object-oriented programming language that is viewed by many as the best language for creating large-scale applications. C++ is a superset of the C language.
- ✓ **C#** - Pronounced **C Sharp**. It is a complete Object-Oriented programming language from Microsoft built into the .NET Framework. First created in the late 1990's was part of Microsoft's whole .NET strategy.
- ✓ **COBOL** - Expanded as Common Business Oriented Language. It is a widely used high level language for developing Business Applications.
- ✓ **Component Pascal** - It's a Pascal derived programming language for development of programming components.
- ✓ **Eiffel** - It is an Object-Oriented programming language which emphasizes the production of robust software.
- ✓ **Forth** - It is both a programming language & a programming environment. It supports shell programming to a high level.
- ✓ **FORTRAN** - Stands for Formula Translator. It's a high level programming language used for scientific computations. It supports plenty of compact notations.

- ✓ **Haskell** - It is a standardized functional programming language with non-strict semantics, named after the logician Haskell Curry. It was created by a committee formed in the 1980s for the express purpose of defining such a language. The latest semi-official language standard is Haskell 98, intended to specify a minimal, portable version of the language for teaching and as a base for future extensions.
- ✓ **Java** - It is an object-oriented programming language developed initially by James Gosling and colleagues at Sun Microsystems. The language, initially called Oak (named after the oak trees outside Gosling's office), was intended to replace C++, although the feature set better resembles that of Objective C. Java should not be confused with JavaScript, which shares only the name and a similar C-like syntax. Sun Microsystems currently maintains and updates Java regularly.
- ✓ **Microsoft JScript** - A scripting language developed by Microsoft to enable Web page designers to design interactive sites. Although it shares many of the features and structures of the full Java language, it was developed independently. Jscript can interact with HTML source code; better enabling Web authors to spice up their sites with dynamic content.
- ✓ **Mercury** - Mercury is a functional/logical programming language based on Prolog, but more useful for real-world programming.
- ✓ **Mondrian** - It is a simple functional scripting language for Internet applications. It is a functional language specifically designed to inter-operate with other languages in an OO environment. Current versions of Mondrian run on .NET. Mondrian also supports ASP.NET, allowing you to embed functional language code in web pages along with C# code.
- ✓ **Oberon** - It is a programming language very much like Modula-2 in syntax but with several interesting features. It's based on OOP concepts and also provides a Windows-based GUI.
- ✓ **Pascal** - A high-level, highly structured, general-purpose programming language. Named after Blaise Pascal.
- ✓ **Perl** - Stands for Practical Extraction and Report Language. It is a language optimized for scanning arbitrary text files, extracting information from those text files, and printing reports based on that information.
- ✓ **Python** - It is an interpreted, interactive, Object-Oriented programming language. Python combines remarkable power with very clear syntax. It has modules, classes, exceptions, very high level dynamic data types, and dynamic typing.
- ✓ **RPG** - Stand for Report Program Generator. It is used for generation of reports from data files, including matching record and sub-total reports. RPG is one of the few languages created for punch card machines that are still in common use today.
- ✓ **Scheme** - It is a statically scoped programming language. It was designed to have an exceptionally unambiguous and simple semantics and few different ways to form expressions. A vast variety of programming paradigms, including imperative, functional, and message passing styles, find convenient expression in Scheme.
- ✓ **Smalltalk** - It is a simple language that uses a simple sub set of human languages, nouns and verbs. Smalltalk was the first, and remains one of the few, pure object systems, which simply mean that everything in a Smalltalk program is an object.
- ✓ **Standard ML** - It is a safe, modular, strict, functional, polymorphic programming language with compile-time type checking and type

inference, garbage collection, exception handling, immutable data types and updatable references, abstract data types, and parametric modules.

✓ **Microsoft Visual Basic** - Most widely used language in the world today! Used for developing Windows based Applications, Windows Services, Remoting Applications, Web Services and Web Applications(using ASP.NET).

Some other popular languages that run on .NET are PHPMono, Vulcan, Zoon, Spry, Synergy, SML, Mono Ruby .NET, Lexico, G#.

Q3. ★Which tools can be used for .NET Development?
A3. The Microsoft .NET Framework SDK is free and includes command-line compilers for C++, C#, and VB.NET and various other utilities to aid development.

SharpDevelop is a free IDE for C# and VB.NET, though this is not used much these days, as its pretty old.

Microsoft Visual Studio Express editions are cut-down versions of Visual Studio, for hobbyist or novice developers and are available as FREE downloads at the Microsoft website. Note that .NET 2.0, 3.0, 3.5, 4.0 Framework may be downloaded along with Visual Studio Express & all versions above Visual Studio Express.

For development of applications, the best tools available are Visual Studio .NET 2010 / 2008 / 2005. Version 2010 goes best with .NET 4, 2008 with .NET 3.5 and 2005 with .NET 2.0. It's worth noting that Visual Studio comes in several recipes such as Ultimate, Premium, Professional, and Express.

Some of the other collaborative platforms for .NET development are Team Foundation Server 2010, Test Professional 2010, Team Explorer Everywhere 2010, and Lightswitch 2011.

Visual Studio 2008 and Visual Studio 2005 are now considered as legacy .NET development environments.

Q4. ★★Does Lightswitch support building .NET applications for the desktop or the cloud?
A4. Lightswitch supports building .NET applications for both the desktop and the cloud.

Q5. ★Explain CLI.
A5. **CLI** – stands for **Common Language Infrastructure**. Microsoft has a piece of shared source; it's the public implementation of ECMA Common Language Infrastructure. This shared code is code-named **Rotor**. It has around three million lines of code. Those who are interested in development of a language that targets the .NET Framework may extensively make use of CLI. The following topics are covered in the Shared Source CLI:

✓ The CLI type system
✓ Component packing & assemblies
✓ Type Loading & JIT Compilation
✓ Managed code & Execution Engine (CLR)

- ✓ Description of Garbage Collection process & memory management
- ✓ The Platform Adaptation Layer (PAL): a portability layer for Win32®, Mac OS® X, and FreeBSD

It's been written by the Microsoft Team that has developed the .NET Framework.

> **Note**: A compiled managed assembly is comprised of IL, Metadata and Manifest.

Q6. ★ Explain CIL.
A6. **CIL** Stands for **Common Intermediate Language**. It's actually a low level human readable language implementation of CLI. All .NET-aware languages compile the source code to an intermediate language called Common Intermediate Language using the language specific compiler. It is also possible to build .NET assemblies directly using CIL using the **ilasm.exe** compiler. This compiler is shipped along with the .NET Framework 2.0 SDK. CIL is the only language that allows access to each aspect of the **CTS**. CIL is the definition of the fundamentals of the .NET framework.

Q7. ★ Explain CTS.
A7. **CTS** - stands for **Common Type Specification**. It is at the core of .NET Framework's cross-language integration, type safety, and high-performance code execution. It defines a common set of types that can be used with many different language syntaxes. Each language *(C#, VB.NET, Managed C++, and so on)* is free to define any syntax it wishes, but if that language is built on the CLR, it will use at least some of the types defined by the CTS.

Q8. ★ Explain Metadata.
A8. **Metadata** - is code that describes the compiled **Intermediate Language** *(IL)*. A .NET language compiler will generate the metadata and store this in the assembly containing the CIL. Metadata describes all class members and classes that are defined in the assembly, and the classes and class members that the current assembly will call from another assembly. The metadata for a method contains the complete description of the method, including the class *(and the assembly that contains the class)*, the return type and all of the method parameters. When the CLR executes CIL, it will check to make sure that the metadata of the called method is the same as the metadata that is stored in the calling method. This ensures that a method can only be called with exactly the correct number of parameters and exactly the correct parameter types.

Q9. ★ Explain CLS. What is the purpose of the CLSCompliant attribute?
A9. **CLS** - **Common Language Specification**. A type that is CLS compliant, may be used across any .NET language. CLS is a set of language rules that defines language standards for a .NET language and types declared in it. While declaring a new type, if we make use of the **[CLSCompliant]** attribute, the type is forced to conform to the rules of CLS.

Q10. ★ Explain Intermediate Language (IL).
A10. **IL** - **Intermediate Language**, is the compiled form of the .NET language source code. When .NET source code is compiled by the language specific compiler *(say we compile C# code using csc.exe)*, it is compiled to a .NET binary, which is platform independent, and this is called Intermediate Language code. The .NET binary also comprises of metadata.

Important: It's important to note here that metadata describes the IL, whereas manifest describes the assembly.

Q11. ★★Explain VES.

A11. **VES - Virtual Execution System**. The Virtual Execution System (VES) provides an environment for executing managed code. It provides direct support for a set of built-in data types, defines a hypothetical machine with an associated machine model and state, a set of control flow constructs, and an exception handling model. To a large extent, the purpose of the VES is to provide the support required to execute the Common Intermediate Language instruction set.

Q12. ★What is CLR in .NET?

A12. **Common Language Runtime *(CLR)*** - It is the implementation of CLI. It is the core runtime engine in the Microsoft .NET Framework for executing applications. The common language runtime supplies managed code with services such as cross-language integration, **code access security** *(CAS)*, object lifetime management, resource management, type safety, pre-emptive threading, metadata services *(type reflection)*, debugging and profiling support. The ASP.NET Framework and Internet Explorer are examples of hosting CLR.

The CLR is a multi-language execution environment. There are currently many compilers being built by Microsoft and other companies. These compilers produce code that executes in the CLR.

The CLR is described as the "execution engine" of .NET. It's this CLR that manages the execution of programs. It provides the environment within which the programs run.

When the .NET program is compiled, the output of the compiler is not an executable file but a file that contains a special type of code called the **Microsoft Intermediate Language** *(MSIL, now called CIL, Common Intermediate Language)*. This MSIL defines a set of portable instructions that are independent of any specific CPU. It's the job of the CLR to translate this Intermediate code into an executable code when the program is executed and allowing the program to run in any environment for which the CLR is implemented. That's how the .NET Framework achieves Portability. This MSIL is turned into executable code using a **JIT** *(Just in Time)* compiler. The process goes like this: When .NET programs are executed, the CLR activates the JIT complier. The JIT compiler converts MSIL into native code on demand basis as each part of the program is needed. Thus the program executes as a native code even though it is compiled into MSIL allowing the program to run as fast as it would if it is compiled to native code, but achieves the portability benefits of MSIL.

Q13. ★★What is CAS in .NET?

A13. **Code Access Security (CAS)** - CAS is the part of the .NET security model that determines whether or not code is allowed to run, and what resources it can use when it is running. For example, it is CAS that will prevent a .NET web applet from formatting your hard disk.

The CAS security policy revolves around two key concepts - **code groups** and **permissions**. Each .NET assembly is a member of a particular code group, and each code group is granted the permissions specified in a named permission set.

For example, using the default security policy, a control downloaded from a web site belongs to the 'Zone - Internet' code group, which adheres to the permissions defined by the 'Internet' named permission set. *(Naturally the 'Internet' named permission set represents a very restrictive range of permissions.)* To view codegroups on our system, use the following command on .NET command interpreter.

caspol -lg

Note the hierarchy of code groups - the top of the hierarchy is the most general *('All code')*, which is then sub-divided into several groups, each of which in turn can be sub-divided. Also note that *(somewhat counter-intuitively)* a sub-group can be associated with a more permissive permission set than its parent. If you want to trust a particular website giving it full rights to the system, use **caspol**. For example, suppose you trust code from www.mydomain.com and you want it have full access to a system, but you want to keep the default restrictions for all other internet sites. To achieve this, you would add a new code group as a sub-group of the 'Zone - Internet' group.

Example: caspol -ag 1.3 -site www.mydomain.com FullTrust

To change the permission, you use the -cg attribute.

To turn off caspol, use caspol -s off

Q14. ★What is a Class Library in .NET?
A14. **Class library** is a major entity of the .NET Framework. This library gives the program access to the runtime environment. The class library consists of lots of prewritten code that all the applications created using .NET aware languages. The code for all the elements such as forms, controls and the rest in VB .NET applications actually comes from the class library.

Code in class libraries may be shared & reused. One of the core .NET libraries is **mscorlib.dll**. .NET language compilers reference this library automatically as it contains core types. A class library contains types that may be used by external applications. A class library may be a DLL or an EXE. Note that the .NET class libraries, even though have a same extension as the old COM Win32 binaries, are very different internally.

Q15. ★Explain Managed code, managed class and managed data in .NET
A15. **Managed Code** - The .NET framework provides lots of core runtime services to the programs that run within it. For example - security & exception handling. Such a code has a minimum level of information. It has metadata associated with it. Such a code is called Managed Code. VB.NET, C#, JS.NET code is managed by default. In order to make C++ code managed, we make use of **managed extensions**, which is nothing but a postfix **_gc** after the class name.

Managed Data - Data that is allocated & freed by the .NET runtime's Garbage collector.

Managed Class - A class whose objects are managed by the CLR's garbage collector. In VC++.NET, classes are not managed. However, they can be managed using managed extensions. This is done using an _gc postfix. A managed C++ class can inherit from VB.NET classes, C# classes, JS.NET classes. A managed class can inherit from only one class. .NET doesn't allow multiple inheritance in managed classes.

Q16. ★What is an assembly in .NET?
A16. **Assembly** - An assembly may be an exe, a dll, an application having an entry point, or a library. It may consist of one or more files. It represents a group of resources, type definitions, and implementation of these types. They may contain references to other assemblies. These resources, types & references are compacted in a block of data called manifest. The manifest is a part of the assembly, which makes it self-describing. Assemblies also increase security of code in .NET. An assembly maybe shared *(public)* or private. The assembly overall comprises of 3 entities: IL, Manifest, and Metadata. Metadata describes IL, whereas Manifest describes the assembly.

An assembly may be created by building the class *(the .vb or .cs file)*, thereby producing its DLL.

Q17. ★What is Reflection in .NET?
A17. **Reflection** - The process of getting the metadata from modules/assemblies. When .NET code is compiled, metadata about the types defined in the modules is produced. These modules are in turn packaged as assemblies. The process of accessing this metadata is called Reflection.

The namespace **System.Reflection** contains classes that can be used for interrogating the types for a module/assembly. We use reflection for examining data type sizes for marshalling across process & machine boundaries.

Reflection is also used to:

- ✓ dynamically invoke methods *(using System.Type.InvokeMember)*
- ✓ dynamically create types at runtime *(using System.Reflection.Emit.TypeBuilder)*.

Q18. ★What are the different types of assemblies in .NET?
A18. An assembly may be **Public** or **Private**. A public assembly is also called a **Shared** Assembly.

Q19. ★What is a satellite assembly?
A19. **A Satellite Assembly** - is an assembly that contains only resources, and no code. The resources are location specific. A satellite assembly is associated with a main assembly, the one that actually contains the code.

Q20. ★What is the difference between a Public Assembly and a Private Assembly?
A20. An assembly is the basic building block in .NET. It is the compiled format of a class that contains **Metadata, Manifest & Intermediate Language code**.

An assembly may either be **Public** or **Private**. A public assembly means the same as **Shared Assembly**.

Private Assembly - This type of assembly is used by a single application. It is stored in the application's directory or the applications sub-directory. There is no version constraint in a private assembly.

Shared Assembly or Public Assembly - A shared assembly has version constraint. It is stored in the **Global Assembly Cache** *(GAC)*. GAC is a repository of shared assemblies maintained by the .NET runtime.

It is located at **C:\Windows\Assembly OR C:\Winnt\Assembly**. The shared assemblies may be used by many applications. To make an assembly a shared assembly, it has to be **strongly named**. In order to share an assembly with many applications, it must have a strong name.

Q21. ★What s a Strong Name assembly? How to create a Strongly Named assembly?
A21. A **Strong Name** assembly is an assembly that has its own identity, through its version and uniqueness.
In order to convert a private assembly to a shared assembly, i.e. to create a strongly named assembly, follow the steps below:

1) Create a strong key using the **sn.exe** tool. This is used to create a cryptographic key pair. The key pair that is generated by the Strong Name tool can be kept in a file or we can store it in your local machine's **Crytographic Service Provider (CSP)**. For this, go to the .NET command interpreter, and type the following...

sn -k C:\samplekey.snk

This will create a strong key and save it to the location C:\samplekey.snk

2) If the key is stored in a file, just like we have done above, we use the attribute **AssemblyKeyFileAttribute**. This belongs to the namespace **System.Reflection.AssemblyKeyFileAttribute**.

If the key was in the CSP, we would make use of
System.Reflection.AssemblyKeyNameAttribute.

Go to the assemblyinfo.vb file of your project. Open this file. Make the following changes in this file:

<assembly: assemblykeyfileattribute("C:\samplekey.snk")>

We may write this in our code as well, like this:

```
Imports System.Reflection
<assembly: assemblykeyfileattribute("C:\samplekey.snk")>
Namespace StrongName
   Public class Sample
   End Class
End Namespace
```

3) Build your project. Your assembly is now strongly named.

Q22. ★★How to install a shared assembly in the global assembly cache (GAC)?
A22. Installing the Shared assembly in the Global Assembly Cache *(GAC)* can be done as follows:

1.   Go to the .NET command interpreter, use the tool **gacutil.exe**

2.   Type the following:
     gacutil /i sampleclass.dll

In order to uninstall the assembly from the GAC, use:

gacutil /u sampleclass.dll

> **Note**: Visual Studio.NET provides a GUI tool for viewing all shared assemblies in the GAC.

Q23. ★What is GAC?
A23. Global Assembly Cache *(GAC)* is the location where shared assemblies are saved. GAC is a repository of shared assemblies in a system, maintained by the .NET runtime. The shared assemblies may be used by many applications. To make an assembly a shared assembly, it has to be strongly named.

> **Note**: Visual Studio.NET provides a GUI tool for viewing all shared assemblies in the GAC.

Q24. ★★Can the garbage collector control the activities of a thread?
A24.**Garbage Collection** - Garbage collection is a heap-management strategy where a run-time component takes responsibility for managing the lifetime of the memory used by objects. This concept is not absolutely new as Java and many other languages/runtimes have used garbage collection. **The garbage collector runs periodically**. It runs through a list of objects that are currently being referenced by an application. All objects that it does not find during this search are ready to be destroyed *(using the finalize method)* and hence free the memory. However, the runtime gets notified of the object that has been destroyed during the next round of the garbage collector's periodic cycle.

In the class **System.GC**, there is a method called **collect()**. This forces the garbage collector to collect all unreferenced objects immediately, thereby giving the developer some control over the garbage collector.

There is a **gcConcurrent** setting that can be set through the applications' .config file. This specifies whether or not the garbage collector performs its activities on a specified thread or not.

> **Tip**: We can view the performance monitor to view the activities of the garbage collector.

Q25. ★What is the role of the IDisposable interface in .NET?
A25. **IDisposable interface** - We implement this interface to a class when we have to work with unmanaged types. For example, an IntPtr member representing an operating system's file handler is actually unmanaged, and in order to destroy it, we make use of the Dispose method by implementing the IDisposable interface. In this case, we override the Finalize method. Note that we make use of Dispose method on those objects which have an uncertain life period, and thus the garbage collector does not finalize them automatically.
We also make use of Dispose method while working with managed code, for example, an object of **System.IO.FileStream** may have an uncertain life, and in order to dispose it, we use the dispose method. Such types of objects are not accessed by the Garbage Collector's Finalizer.

Q26. ★What is Serialization in .NET?
A26. **Serialization** - The process of converting an object into a stream of bytes. This stream of bytes can be persisted. **Deserialization** is an opposite process, which involves converting a stream of bytes into an object. Serialization is used usually during remoting *(while transporting objects)* and while saving file objects & database objects.

Q27. ★What is a class attribute in .NET?
A27. **Class Attributes** - Is a kind of property attached with a class. It allows some data to be attached to a class or method. This data becomes part of the metadata for the class, and *(like other class metadata)* can be accessed via reflection. An example of a metadata attribute is [serializable], which can be attached to a class. That means that instances of the class can be serialized.

Example (C#):

```
[Serializable]
Public Class clsAlcohol
{ ... }
```

Q28. ★What is a thread? How to use and create a thread in .NET? Explain the AddressOff operator.
A28. **Threads** - When we want to run one or more instances of a method, we make use of threading. Suppose we have a method like this:

Example (VB.NET):

```
Private Sub OnGoingProcess()
  Dim i As Integer = 1
  Do While True
   ListBox1.Items.Add("Waiter, please pour peg number: " + i + " please! ")
   i += 1
  Loop
End Sub

Dim t As Thread
t = New Thread(AddressOf Me.OnGoingProcess)
t.Start()
```

The **AddressOf** operator creates a delegate object to the method. A delegate within VB.NET is a type-safe, object-oriented function pointer. After the thread has been instantiated, you begin the execution of the code by calling the **Start()** method of the thread. After the thread is started, you have some control over the state of it by using the methods of the thread object. You can pause a thread's execution by calling the **Thread.Sleep()** method. This method takes an integer value that determines how long the thread should sleep. If you wanted to slow down the addition of items to the listbox in the example above, place a call to the sleep method in this code:

```
Private Sub OnGoingProcess()
Dim i As Integer = 1
Do While True
   ListBox1.Items.Add("This is peg number: " + i)
   i += 1
   Thread.CurrentThread.Sleep(2000)
   Loop
End Sub
```

You can also place a thread into the sleep state for an indeterminate amount of time by calling **Thread.Sleep()** method. To interrupt this sleep you can call the **Thread.Interrupt()** method. Similar to Sleep and Interrupt are **Suspend** and **Resume**. Suspend allows you to block a thread until another thread calls **Thread.Resume()**. **The difference between Sleep and Suspend** is that the latter does not immediately place a thread in the wait state. The thread does not suspend until the .NET runtime determines that it is in a safe place to suspend it. Sleep will immediately place a thread in a wait state. Lastly, Thread.Abort stops a thread from executing. In our simple example, we would want to add another button on the form that allows us to stop the process. To do this all we would have to do is call the **Thread.Abort()** method as follows:

```
Private Sub Button2_Click(ByVal sender As System.Object, _
   ByVal e As System.EventArgs) Handles Button2.Click
   t.Abort()
End Sub
```

This is where the power of **multithreading** can be seen. The UI seems responsive to the user because it is running in one thread and the background process is running in another thread. The cancel button immediately responds to the user's click event and processing stops. The next example shows a rather simple situation. Multithreading has many complications that you have to work out when you program. One issue that you may run into is passing data to and from the procedure passed to the constructor of the Thread class. That is to say, the procedure you want to kick off on another thread cannot be passed any parameters, and you cannot return data from that procedure. This is because the procedure you pass to the thread constructor cannot have any parameters or return value. To get around this, wrap your procedure in a class where the parameters to the method are written as fields of the class. A simple example of this would be if you had a procedure that calculated the square of a number:

```
Function Square(ByVal Value As Double) As Double
Return Value * Value
End Function
```

To make this procedure available to be used in a new thread, you would wrap it in a class:

```
Public Class SquareClass Public Value As Double Public Square As Double

  Public Sub CalcSquare()
    Square = Value * Value
  End Sub
End Class
```

Use this code to start the CalcSquare procedure on a new thread. See the following code:

```
Private Sub Button1_Click(ByVal sender As System.Object, _
  ByVal e As System.EventArgs) Handles Button1.Click
    Dim oSquare As New SquareClass()
    t = New Thread(AddressOf oSquare.CalcSquare)
    oSquare.Value = 30
    t.Start()
End Sub
```

Notice that after the thread is started, you do not inspect the square value of the class, because it is not guaranteed to have executed once you call the start method of the thread. There are a few ways to retrieve values back from another thread. The easiest way is to raise an event when the thread is complete. There is another method in the next section on thread synchronization. The following code adds the event declarations to the SquareClass.

```
Public Class SquareClass
    Public Value As Double
    Public Square As Double
    Public Event ThreadComplete(ByVal Square As Double)
    Public Sub CalcSquare()
    Square = Value * Value
    RaiseEvent ThreadComplete(Square)
  End Sub
End Class
```

Catching the events in the calling code has not changed much from VB6; you still declare the variables WithEvents and handle the event in a procedure. The part that has changed is the place where you declare the procedure that handles the event using the Handles keyword.

```
Private Sub Button1_Click(ByVal sender As System.Object, _
  ByVal e As System.EventArgs) Handles Button1.Click
    oSquare = New SquareClass()
    t = New Thread(AddressOf oSquare.CalcSquare)
    oSquare.Value = 30
    t.Start()
End Sub

Sub SquareEventHandler(ByVal Square As Double) _
  Handles oSquare.ThreadComplete
```

```
MsgBox("The square is " & Square)
End Sub
```

The one thing to note with this method is that the procedure handling the event, in this case SquareEventHandler, will run within the thread that raised the event. It does not run within the thread from which the form is executing.

Q29. ★What is globalization in .NET?
A29. **Globalization** refers to the process with which an application or software is designed and developed so as to make it run across all platforms and all sites with minimum or no modification to the software application. The software is very easy to customize so as to suit to the location-specific conditions and it is also capable of providing information based on the varied inputs and the location-specific operating system.

There are two processes in Globalization and they are **customization** or **localization** of the application and internationalizing the application codes so as to meet the standards of the local culture and other related matters.

In the **internationalization** process, the application code base is the same and the efforts will be on jobs such as **translating, storing, retrieving** and to make the application user friendly for the selected locale. In any given place the culture and the language will always be different and besides this, you should also take into account the other factors such as time zone, normal date pattern usage, cultural and language environments, currencies, telephone numbers, and so many other factors that are specific to the locale. In globalization the process of internationalization empowers you to remove from the code base and the presentation layer all the contents and make you to use only a single presentation layer and single code base with a common contents that can suit any culture. The internationalization process will aid us to keep all the contents in a common place with an idea of making it easily accessible by the program codes and the results can easily be populated all over presentation layer and the application with ease and efficiency.

Moreover, the internationalization process also enables you to store the contents and all the collected inputs from the user in a user friendly format and in a highly secured manner without compromising any standards pertaining to the local culture. The internationalization process is one step before any attempt for localizing the application to suit to the local needs.

With the help of the localization process of globalization, you can make your application adaptable to the various location specific conditions and it will be easy for you to translate and re-format our application to suit to our new location and that too without changing any of the codes. Further, you may make use of the process for rectifying any of the reported bugs and for fine tuning the application for running efficiently. The globalization process also makes use of the locally prevailing information on culture where the software or the application is to be installed and maintained. The locational details and the language used in that particular area constitutes the culture information. For working with any culture based information, the **System.Globalization, System.Resources** and **System.Threading** are the available namespaces.

Out of the various namespaces, the **System.Globalization** namespace constitute classes that are used to hold information related to region or country, the local language used, the type of calendars, the date format used, the numbers, the currency, etc., all in a meticulously arranged fashion. All these classes are used while developing the globalized *(internationalized)* applications. You can use advanced globalization functionalities with the assistance of classes such as **StringInfo** and **TextInfo** classes, and the various functionalities that include text element processing and surrogate support systems.

The **System.Resources** namespace constitutes interfaces and classes that are very helpful for developers and maintenance experts in creating, storing, retrieving, and managing various resources used in the application that are culture and location-specific.

The **System.Threading** namespace constitutes interfaces and classes that aid in multithreaded programming. The classes that are used in this type of System.Threading namespace are also useful in accessing data, and for synchronization of thread activities.

Q30. ★★What are Generations in Garbage Collector?
A30. Generations in the Garbage Collector are a way of enhancing the **garbage collection** performance. In .NET, all resources are allocated space *(memory)* from the heap. Objects are automatically freed from the managed heap when they are no longer required by the application.

When objects are no longer being used by the application, the .NET runtime's garbage collector performs the task of collection, to determine the status of the objects. Necessary operations are performed to relieve the memory, in case the object is no longer in use. This is identified by the GC by examining the metadata of the object. For this, the GC has to know the location of the roots that represent the object. Roots are actually the location of the object on the managed heap. There are two types of memory references, strong & weak. When a root references an object, it is said to be a strong reference as the object is being pointed to by application code. The other type of object that is not being referenced by the application code is called the weak reference, and this may be collected by the GC. However, this may still be accessed by the application code if required. But for the application to access the weakly referenced object, this has to be converted to a strong *reference (and note that this has to be done before the GC collects the weakly referenced object).*

So what are Generations in the GC? It's a feature of the GC that enhances its performance.

> **Important:** There are three Generations: 0, 1 and 2.

Generation 0 - When an object is initialized, it's in generation 0. These are new objects that have never been played around with by the GC. As and when more objects get created, the process of Garbage Collection is invoked by the CLR.

Generation 1 - The objects that survive the garbage collection process are considered to be in generation 1. These are the old objects.

Generation 2 - As more new objects get created and added to the memory, the new objects are added to generation 0; the generation 1 old objects become older, and so are considered to be in generation 2.

Generation 2 is the highest level generation in the garbage collection process. Any further garbage collection process occurring causes the level 1 objects promoted to level 2, and the level 2 objects stay in level 2 itself, as this generation level is the highest level.

So what is the importance & use of the generations concept? It's actually the priority the GC gives to objects while freeing objects from the heap. During every GC cycle, the objects in the Generation 0 are scanned first; this is followed by Generation 1 and then 2. The idea behind a sequential generation is that the generation 0 objects are usually short term objects that need to be freed first. The newer an object, the shorter its life. The older an object, the longer its life.

This process also helps in categorizing the memory heap as to where the de-allocation needs to be done first and where next.

Q31. ★★★How to call COM components from .NET? What is interoperability?
A31. COM components & .NET components have a different internal architecture. For both of them to communicate with each other, inter-operation feature is required, this feature is called interoperability. Enterprises that have written their business solutions using the old native COM technology need a way for re-using these components in the new .NET environment.

.NET components communicate with COM using a **Runtime Callable Wrapper** *(RCW)*.

To use a COM component,

- ✓ Right click the Project & click on Add References.
- ✓ Select the COM tab
- ✓ Select the COM component

Another way of using a COM component is using the **tblimp.exe** tool *(Type Library Import)*. Further, using the COM component directly in the code may be achieved by using **System.Runtime.InteropServices** namespace. This contains a class TypeLib Converter which provides methods to convert COM classes and interface in to assembly metadata. If the COM component does not have a Type Library, then custom wrappers need to be created. Once the COM wrapper is created, it has to be registered in the registry.

Q32. ★★★How to call .NET component from COM?
A32. In case a .NET component needs to be used in COM, we make use of **COM Callable Wrapper** *(CCW)*. Following are the different approaches to implement it:

- ✓ Explicitly declare interfaces.
- ✓ The second way to create CCW is by using InteropServices attributes. Here interfaces are created automatically.

Following are the different types of class attributes:

- ✓ **None** - No class interface is generated for the class. This is default setting when you do not specify anything.
- ✓ **AutoDispatch** - Interface that supports IDispatch is created for the class. However, no type information is produced.
- ✓ **AutoDual** - A dual interface is created for the class. Typeinfo is produced and made available in the type library.

In the source code below, you have used the third attribute.

Example (VB.NET):

```
Imports System.Runtime.InteropServices
 <ClassInterfaceAttribute(ClassInterfaceType.AutoDual)> _
 Public Class ClsCompliant
End Class
```

Other than the class attributes defined, there are other attributes using which you can govern other parts of an assembly. For example, "GuidAttribute" allows you to specify the GUID, "ComVisibleAttribute" can be used to hide .NET types from COM etc.

CHAPTER 3 – C#

Q1. ★What does the modifier protected internal in C# mean?
A1. The **Protected Internal** access specifier can be accessed by members of the Assembly or the inheriting class, and of course, within the class itself.

In VB.NET, the equivalent of protected internal is **protected friend**.

The access of this modifier is limited to the current assembly or the types derived from the defining class in the current assembly.

Q2. ★Can multiple data types be stored in System.Array?
A2. This is tricky! First understand what is an **array** all about? An array is a collection of items of the same type that is grouped together and encompassed within an array object. The array object, or the **System.Array** object to be precise, is derived from the System.Object class. It is thus, stored in the form of a heap in the memory.

An array may be of single dimensional, multi-dimensional or jagged (a jagged array means an array within an array).

A group of items when assigned values within braces implicitly derive from the **System.Array** class. See example below written in C#...

Example (C#):

```
int[] testIntArray = new int[4] { 2, 3, 4, 5 };
Object[] testObjArray = new Object[5] { 32, 22, 23, 69, 75 };
```

Ideally an array should contain a single data type. But still in case there is a requirement to place data of different data types in a specific array, then in such a scenario, the data elements should be declared as an **object** type. When this is done, then each element may point ultimately to a different data type. See the code example below:

Example (VB.NET:

```
Dim allTypes As Object() = New Object() {}
```

'In this kind of scenario, the performance may tend to slow down, as data conversions may take place.
'In case a value type is converted to reference type, then boxing and unboxing occurs

```
Dim studentTable(2) As Object
studendTable(0) = "Vishal Khanna"
studentTable(1) = 28
studentTable(2) = #9/1/1978#
```

'To get these values of these varying datatypes, their values are converted to their original data type

```
Dim myAge As Integer = CInt(studentTable(1))
Dim lastDateIHadWhisky as Date = CDate(studentTable(2))
```

Q3. ★How to sort array elements in descending order in C#?

A3. Elements of an array may not be sorted by default. To sort them in descending order, the **Sort()** method is first called. Next, to descend the order, call the **Reverse()** method.

Q4. ★What is the use of "throw" keyword in C#?

A4. The **throw** keyword is used to throw an exception programmatically in C#. In .NET, there is an in-built technique to manage & throw exceptions. In C#, there are three keywords that are used to implement exception handling. These are the **try**, **catch** and **finally** keywords. In case an exception has to be implicitly thrown, then the **throw** keyword is used. See the example below, for throwing an exception programmatically...

C# Example:

```
class SomeClass
{
public static void Main()
{
  try
  {
    throw new DivideByZeroException("Invalid Division Occured");
  }
  catch(DivideByZeroException e)
  {
    Console.WriteLine("Exception - Divide by Zero" );
  }
}
}
```

Q5. ★Can we put multiple catch blocks in a single try statement in C#?

A5. Yes. Multiple catch blocks may be put in a try block. See the example below, to understand how multiple catch blocks are used in C#.

Example (C#):
```
class ClassA
{
public static void Main()
{
  int y = 0;
  try
  {
    val = 100/y;
    Console.WriteLine("Line not executed");
  }
  catch(DivideByZeroException ex)
  {
    Console.WriteLine("DivideByZeroException" );
  }
  catch(Exception ex)
  {
    Console.WritLine("Some Exception" );
  }
  finally
```

```
  {
    Console.WriteLine("This Finally Line gets executed always");
  }
  Console.WriteLine("Result is {0}",val);
  }
}
```

Q6. ★How to add a ReadOnly property in C#?

A6. **Property** - A property is an entity that describes the features of an object. A property is a piece of data contained within a class that has an exposed interface for reading and writing. Looking at that definition, you might think you could declare a public variable in a class and call it a property. While this assumption is somewhat valid, the true technical term for a public variable in a class is a field. The key **difference between a field and a property** is in the inclusion of an interface. We make use of **Get** and **Set** keywords while working with properties. We prefix the variables used within this code block with an underscore. **Value** is a keyword that holds the value which is being retrieved or set. See code below to set a property as **ReadOnly**. If a property does not have a set accessor, it becomes a ReadOnly property.

Example (C#):

```
public class ClassA
{
  private int length = 0;
  public ClassA(int propVal)
  {
    length = propVal;
  }
  public int length
  {
    get
    {
      return length;
    }
  }
}
```

Q7. ★How to prevent a class from being inherited? What is 'Sealed' in C#?

A7. In order to prevent a class in C# from being inherited, the **sealed** keyword is used. Thus a sealed class may not serve as a base class of any other class. It is also obvious that a sealed class cannot be an abstract class. Checkout the code example below:

Example (C#):

```
sealed class clsAlcohol
{
  public int thirtyml;
  public int sixtyml;
}
```

No class can inherit from ClassA defined above. The instances of ClassA may be created and its members may then be accessed, but nothing like the code below is possible:

```
class clsRum: clsAlcohol {} // Error
```

Q8. ★★How to inherit the class, but not the method inside it in C#? What is a sealed method in C#? Can a method in C# be sealed? How to create a sealed method in C#?
A8. If a method is not to be inherited, but the class is, then the method is sealed. It becomes a **sealed method** of a class. It is important to note here that in C#, a method may not be implicitly declared as sealed. This means that a method cannot be sealed directly. A method in C# can be sealed only when the method is an overriden method. Once the overriden method is declared as sealed, it will not be further overriding of this method. See code sample below, where an overriden method is sealed.

Example (C#):
```
class clsAlcohol
{
    public int thirtyml;
    public int sixtyml;

    public virtual void Pour()
    {
        Console.WriteLine("Thanks for pouring. Cheers!");
    }
}
class clsWhisky : clsAlcohol
{
    public override sealed void Pour()
    {
        Console.WriteLine("This bottle is sealed. How will you pour?");
    }
}
```

Q9. ★Can we inherit multiple interfaces in C#?
A9. Yes. Multiple interfaces may be inherited in C#.

> **Note**: When a class and multiple interfaces are to be inherited, then the class name should be written first, followed by the names of the interfaces.

See code example below, on how to inherit multiple interfaces in C#.

Example (C#):

```
class clsWhisky : clsAlcohol, IScotchWhisky, IDesiBrand, IIrishWhisky
{
    //...Some code in C#
}
```

Q10. ★What are the different ways of overloading methods in C#? What is function overloading in C#?
A10. Before knowing the different methods of overloading in C#, lets first clear out what exactly overloading is. **Overloading** is the OOPs concept of using a method or a class in different styles by modifying the signature of the parameters in it.

In order to achieve overloading, there may be several techniques applied. There are different types of overloading like Operator Overloading, Function Overloading etc.

Function overloading may be achieved by changing the order of parameters in a function, by changing the types passed in the function, and also by changing the number of parameters passed in a function. See code sample below to see types of overloading.

Example (C#):

```
//Define a method below
public void fnDrink(int thirtyml, double sixtyml) {
   .....
}
//change the order of parameters
public void fnDrink (double patiyaala, int onTheRocks) {
  //.......Some code in C#
}
//Similarly, we may change the number of parameters in fnProcess and alter the behavior
```

Q11. ★How to call a specific base constructor in C#?
A11. What is a **Constructor?** - It is a method that gets invoked when an instance of a class is created. In case a class has plenty of constructors, i.e. there are plenty of overloaded constructors, it is still possible to invoke a specific base constructor. But there is a special way, as explicit calls to a base constructor are not possible in C#. See code below:

Example (C#):

```
public class dotnetClass
{
public dotnetClass()
{
  // The constructor method here
}
  // Write the class members here
}

//Sample code below shows how to overload a constructor
public class dotnetClass
{
  public dotnetClass()
  {
   // This constructor is without a parameter
   // Constructor #1
```

```
}
public dotnetClass(string name)
{
  // This constructor has 1 parameter.
  // Constructor #2
}
}
```

This constructor gets executed when an object of this class is instantiated. This is possible in C#. Calling a specific constructor will depend on how many parameters, and what parameters match a specific constructor. Note that a compile time error may get generated when 2 constructors of the same signature are created.

We may make use of the **this** keyword and invoke a constructor. See code example below.

```
this("One drink is anyways on me today. What about Bacardi White?");
//This will call Constructor #2 above
```

What is the use of the base keyword?

Suppose we have a derived class named dotnetderivedclass. If this derived class is to invoke the constructor of a base class, we make use of the base keyword. See the code example below on how to use a base keyword to invoke the base class constructor.

```
public class dotnetClass
{
public dotnetClass()
{
// The 1st base class constructor defined here
}

public dotnetClass(string Name)
{
// The 2nd base class constructor defined here
}
}

public class dotnetderivedclass : dotnetClass
// A class is being inherited out here
{
public dotnetderivedclass()
{
// dotnetderivedclass 1st constructor defined here
}

public dotnetderivedclass(string name):base(name)
{
// dotnetderivedclass 2nd constructor defined here
```

```
}
}
```

Note that we have used the base keyword in the sample code above. The sequence of execution of the constructors will be as follows:

public dotnetClass() method → public dotnetderivedclass() method

The above sequence triggers when there is no initializer to the base class, and thus it triggers the parameterless base class constructor. The other base class constructor may also get invoked when we pass a parameter while defining it.

Q12. ★★What are generics in C#?
A12. 'Generics' in C# is a new innovative feature through which classes and methods in C# may be designed in such a way that the rules of a type are not followed until it is declared. The generics feature in C# has been introduced with version 2.0 of the .NET Framework. Using generics, a class template may be declared. This template may follow any type as required at runtime. The class behavior is later governed by the type that we pass to the class. Once the type is passed, the class behaves depending on the type passed to this generic class. A generic class is type safe at runtime.

Q13. ★What is the use of the main() function in C#?
A13. Every executable C# application must contain a class defining a Main() method that signifies the entry point of the application. Note that the Main() method is of the access type **public** by nature. Moreover, it is also **static**. See example below:

Example (C#):

```
using System;
class Question
{
 public static int Main(string[] args)
 {
  Console.Writeline("Another peg please!");
  Console.Readline();
  return 0;
 }
}
```

A public member is accessible from other types. The main() method is set as static so that it may be invoked at class level itself, without the need of creating an instance of it. The single parameter is an array of strings that may contain any number of incoming command line arguments.

Q14. ★Are C# Keywords in lowercase or uppercase?
A14. All C# keywords are in lowercase.

Namespaces, Types and Members have their first character in uppercase.

Q15. ★What is the use of Console.Readline() in C#?

A15. Using the Console.Readline() method means that the command prompt launched by Visual Studio remains visible during an application session until the ENTER key is pressed by the user.

Q16. ★★Can we set the specifier of the main() method in C# as private?
A16. Yes. When the access specifier is set as private for the Main() method, then other assemblies may not invoke this class' Main() method as the starting point of the application. The startup scope gets limited to the class in context itself. See code below:

Example (C#):

```
private static void Main()
{
    //This code isn't invoked automatically by other assemblies
}
```

Q17. ★★Can we set different types of parameters & return-types in the main() method"?
A17. Yes. The Main() method may easily be played around with by developers by passing different parameters and setting different return types. See the code below that demonstrates different ways the Main() method may be implemented:

Example (C#):

```
(1)
public static void Main(string[] args)
{
    //NO return type, the argument is an array of strings
}

(2)
public static int Main(string[] args)
{
    //Return type is int, argument is an array of strings
}

(3)
public static int Main()
{
    //Return type is int, NO arguments
}

(4)
public static void Main()
{
    //Return type is void, NO arguments
}
```

Q18. ★What is the use of GetCommandLineArgs() method?
A18. The **GetCommandLineArgs()** method is used to access the command line arguments. The return value of this method is an array of strings. It is a method of the **System.Environment** class. See the code example below:

Example (C#):

```csharp
public static int Main(string[] args)
{
  string[] strArgs = System.Environment.GetCommandLineArgs();
  Console.WriteLine("Arguments {0}", strArgs[0]);
}
```

Q19. ★What is the use of System.Environment class?
A19. The class **System.Environment** is used to retrieve information about the operating system. Some of the static members of this class are as follows:

- ✓ **Environment.OSVersion** - Gets the version of the operating system
- ✓ **Environment.GetLogicalDrives()** - method that returns the drives
- ✓ **Environment.Version** - returns the .NET version running the application
- ✓ **Environment.MachineName** - Gets name of the current machine
- ✓ **Environment.Newline** - Gets the newline symbol for the environment
- ✓ **Environment.ProcessorCount** - returns number of processors on current machine
- ✓ **Environment.SystemDirectory** - returns complete path to the System Directory
- ✓ **Environment.UserName** - returns name of the entity that invoked the application

Q20. ★Why is the 'new' keyword used for instantiating an object in .NET?
A20. The **new** keyword instructs the .NET compiler to instantiate a new object, with appropriate number of bytes *(depending on the type)* for the object. It gathers required memory from the managed heap.

Q21. ★What are the default values for bool, int, double, string, char, reference-type variables?
A21. When the objects of the following types are declared, then they have a default value during declaration. The following table shows the default value for each type:

Type	Default Value
bool	false
int	0
double	0
string	null
char	'\0'
Reference Type	null

Q22. ★★Why does the compiler throw an error when variables are declared with an initial value?
A22. The compiler throws an error when a variable is declared without an initial value, when the declaration is within a member scope. The variables do not receive default value when they are declared within a scope.

Note that if the variable is used as an output parameter, this variable does not need to be assigned an initial value.

Q23. ★How to declare a constant variable in C#? What is the use of the const keyword?
A23. If a variable needs to have a fixed value that may not be changed across the application's life, then it may be declared with the **const** keyword. The value assigned to a constant variable *(using the const keyword)* must be known at the time of compilation.

Q24. ★★In C#, can we create an object of reference type using const keyword?
A24. No. A constant member may not be created of an object that is of reference type, because its value is decided dynamically at runtime.

Q25. ★★What are the different parameter modifiers available in C#? What is a parameter modifier?
A25. **Parameter modifiers** in C# are entities that controls the behavior of the arguments passed in a method. Following are the different parameter modifiers in C#:

1) **None** - if there is no parameter modifier with an argument, it is passed by value, where the method receives a copy of the original data.

2) **out** - argument is passed by reference. The argument marked with "out" modifier needs to be assigned a value within this function, otherwise a compiler error is returned.

Example (C#):

```
public void multiply(int a, int b, out int prod)
{
 prod = a * b;
}
```

Here, note that prod is assigned a value. If not done so, then a compile time error is returned.

3) **params**- This modifier gives the permission to set a variable number of identical datatype arguments.

Note that a method may have **only one** "params" modifier. The params modifier needs to be in the **last argument.**

Example (C#):

```
static int totalpegs(params int[] pegs)
{
 int qty = 0;
 for(int x=0; x
 qty +=pegs[x];
```

```
  return qty;
}
```

Further, from the calling function, we may pass the scores of each batsman as below...

```
qty = totalpegs(12,36,0,5,83,25,26);
```

4) **ref** - The argument is given a value by the caller, where data is passed by reference. This value may optionally be reset in the called method. Note that even if no value is set in the called method for the **ref** attribute, no compiler error is raised.

Q26. ★ What is an interface in C#?

A26. An **Interface** is a named collection of semantically similar abstract members or functions. A class or a structure may follow a behaviour that is prescribed by an interface. The keyword **interface** is used to create an interface. Note that while defining members inside an interface, there is no need to specify the access specifier, as they are **public** by default.

Example (C#):

```
public interface IAlcohol
{
  long int Beer_Price;
}
```

As a convention, interfaces in .NET are prefixed with an "I" in uppercase, as a good programming practice.

Methods inside an interface do not have a body. They only signify that such a method should exist in the implementing class or structure.

Classes that display a common set of features, such as having similar types of member variables or member functions, are designed in such a way that they implement a common interface.

Q27. ★ How to implement an interface in C#?

A27. An interface may be implemented using the keyword **"implements"** in VB.NET, and using a colon in C#. See code C# example below:

Example (C#):

```
interface IBooks
{
   long int Cost { get; } //Interface property
}
//ComputerBooks is a class that implements an Interface IBooks
public class ComputerBooks : IBooks
{
  // Implementation of the property
```

```
public long int Cost
{
    get { return 100; } //Read only value
  }
}
```

Q28. ★★★How to figure out at runtime, whether an object of a class, implements an interface or not?

A28. If a class implements an interface, there must be a way to find out at run time, whether the object of this class implements an interface or not. There are three ways to do this:

1) Explicit cast - A try catch block may be weaved in the C# code, to figure out whether a class supports an interface or not. This may be done by explicitly casting an object to the interface itself. See code below to understand how this works:

```
//Say we have an interface by the name IBooks
//Let there be a class by the name MathsBooks, which may or may not implement IBooks
//Lets find out using a try catch block, how we may figure this out...
MathsBooks mb = new MathsBooks();
IBooks ib;
try
{
  ib = (IBooks)mb; //Here, we are explicitly casting the object mb to IBooks
  Messagebox.Show("It works, MathsBooks does implement from IBooks");
}
catch(InvalidCastException ex)
{
  Messagebox.Show(ex.Message);
  Messagebox.Show("It doesn't work, MathsBooks does not implement from IBooks");
}
```

2) Using the "as" keyword - getting a reference to an interface

Using the "as" keyword to check whether an object supports an interface or not, is pretty simple. For this, an instance of the interface needs to be set to the class's object, which is internally casted to the interface using the "is" keyword. See code example below for more clarity:

Example (C#):

```
MathsBooks mb = new MathsBooks();
IBooks ib = mb as IBooks;
if(ib == null)
{
  Messagebox.Show("The class MathsBooks does not implement the interface IBooks");
}
else
{
  Messagebox.Show("The class MathsBooks does implement the interface IBooks");
}
```

2) Using the "is" keyword - getting a reference to an interface

This is perhaps, the simplest way to check for an interface reference. If an interface is being implemented by an object of a class, the "is" keyword may be used. This may be checked in combination with an if statement. See code example below:

```
MathsBooks mb = MathsBooks();
if(mb is IBooks)
{
    Messagebox.Show("The class MathsBooks does implement the interface IBooks");}
}
```

Q29. ★★**Which interfaces belong to the System.Collections namespace? Which classes belong to the System.Collections namespace?**
A29. Objects deriving from System.Collections have the ability to resize, depending on the size of the values in the container, unlike objects deriving from System.Array. They have methods to sort, reverse, clear, enumerate the entities inside them. Note that System.Collections is a very important class and is very commonly used in .NET.

The following are the interfaces that belong to the System.Collections namespace:

- ✓ **ICollection** - this interface defines generic properties for a class
- ✓ **IComparer** - this interface allows two or more objects to be compared
- ✓ **IDictionary** - this interface defines an object in a series of name - value pairs
- ✓ **IDictionaryEnumerator** - provides an enumerated value to the types that implement IDictionary interface
- ✓ **IEnumerable** - this interface allows return of an IEnumerator interface for an object
- ✓ **IEnumerator** - This interface allows the iteration of types inside it
- ✓ **IHashCodeProvider** - This interface allows returning of the hashcode for the implementing type with the use of hash-based algorithms
- ✓ **IKeyComparer** - This interface has been introduced in .NET 2.0 Framework. It is a fusion of the functionalities and features that come in the IComparer and IHashCodeProvider interfaces.
- ✓ **IList** - This interface allows addition, removal and indexing of items in an object list. Types implementing this may be read-only and of fixed size.

The following are the classes that belong to the System.Collections namespace:

- ✓ **ArrayList** - This type may be used to contain any object. The size of this object is variable, and is dynamically decided depending on the number of entities added or removed from it. It implements IList, ICollection, IEnumerable and ICloneable interfaces.
- ✓ **Hashtable** - This type may be used to contain any object, with each entity identifiable by a unique numeric key. If a custom type is stored inside a Hashtable object, then it must override the System.Object.GetHashCode() method. It implements the IDictionary, ICollection, IEnumerable, ICloneable interfaces.

✓ **Queue** - This type is used to store entities in a manner so as to enable First-in-First-out processing. It implements ICollection, IEnumerable, ICloneable interfaces.

✓ **SortedList** - The entities inside this type are sorted like in a dictionary. Also, the entities in this type of object may be accessed using an index. This implements the IDictionary, ICollection, IEnumerable and ICloneable interfaces.

✓ **Stack** - This type is used to store entities in a manner so as to enable Last-in-First-out processing. It implements ICollection, IEnumerable, ICloneable interfaces.

Q30. ★Is it possible to store multiple data types in a System.Array object?
A30. No.

Q31. ★What is the difference between System.Array.CopyTo() and System.Array.Clone() methods?
A31. Well, the **System.Array.CopyTo()** method is used to perform a deep copy of the array, whereas the **System.Array.Clone()** method creates a shallow copy.

Q32. ★How can we sort the elements of the array in descending order?
A32. This is simple and can be done by calling the **sort()** method, followed by the **reverse()** method.

Q33. ★Which object in .NET allows the fetching of data by using a unique key?
A33. The Hashtable object. A Hashtable maintains a key-value pair.

Q34. ★Does the finally block execute in case an exception doesn't take place?
A34. Yes, the code in the 'finally' block is called, even if the exception hasn't taken place.

Q35. ★Can multiple catch blocks be fired?
A35. This is not possible. When the right catch block is fired, the control is passed to the finally block.

Q36. ★What namespaces are necessary to create a localized application?
A36. System.Globalization and System.Resources.

Q37. ★What is the difference between the following types of comments: //, /* */ comments and /// comments?
A37. Well, // is used for Single-line comments, /* */ is used for multi-line comments, and /// is used for XML documentation comments.

Q38. ★How do you generate documentation from a C# file commented properly, with a command-line compiler?
A38. This can be simply done by compiling it with a /doc switch.

Q39. ★What's the difference between the <c> and <code> XML documentation tags?

A39. These tags are used to create single line code examples and multiple-line code examples in the documentation.

Q40. ★Is XML a case-sensitive language?
A40. Yes, XML is case-sensitive. To understand better, <Wine> and <wine> are different elements.

Q41. ★Which debugging tools come along with the .NET SDK?
A41. The following tools come along the .NET SDK:

- ✓ CorDBG – a command-line debugger
- ✓ DbgCLR – a graphic debugger.

Further, Visual Studio .NET uses the **DbgCLR**. To use **CorDbg**, you must compile the original C# file using the /debug switch.

Q42. ★What is the name of the C# compiler file?
A42. It Is called **csc.exe**

Q43. ★★What does the "This" window display in the debugger?
A43. The "This" window points to the object that is pointed to by the 'this' reference. The specified object's instance data is shown.

Q44. ★★What is the assert() method used for?
A44. In a debug compilation, the assert() method takes a boolean condition as a parameter, and displays an error dialog, if the condition is false. The program proceeds without any interruption if the condition is true.

Q45. ★What is the use of 5 tracing levels in System.Diagnostics.TraceSwitcher?
A45. Because the tracing dumps can be quite verbose, if an application is running non-stop, the application might run the risk of overloading the memory. So these five levels (from None to Verbose) allow to fine-tune the tracing activities.

Q46. ★★★Where is the output of the TextWriterTraceListener redirected?
A46. This output is redirected to the Console or a text file, depending on the parameter passed to the constructor.

Q47. ★How do we debug an ASP.NET Web application?
A47. Though this is handled by the Visual Studio environment, leaving the background processes hidden from the developer, it is always better to know what exactly is happening behind the scenes. This is basically done by attaching the **aspnet_wp.exe** process to the **DbgCLR** debugger.

Q48. ★★Can you change the value of a variable while debugging a C# application? If yes, how?
A48. Well yes, if you are debugging using Visual Studio.NET, you simply need to go to the Immediate window.

Q49. ★What is the role of the DataReader class in ADO.NET connections?
A49. The DataReader class returns a read-only dataset from the data source when the command is executed.

Q50. ★What does the term immutable mean?
A50. The term **immutable** basically means that the data value may not be changed. The variable value may be changed, but the original immutable data value was discarded and a new data value was created in the memory.

CHAPTER 4 – ASP.NET FAQs

Q1. ★How to redirect a page to another page?

A1. This is a common question asked in interviews. The **Response** object has a famous **Redirect** method that is used most widely to transfer a web page visitor from one page to another page.

Syntax of Response.Redirect:

```
Response.Redirect("GoToTheCocktailPage.aspx")
```

There is another famous method called **Transfer** method, and this belongs to the **Server** object.

Syntax of Server.Transfer ...

```
Server.Transfer("GoToTheCocktailPage.aspx")
```

Q2. ★How to pass values between pages?

A2. Every interviewer will expect this from you. There are several methods to pass values from one page to another page. Described below are few methods to pass values between pages:

QueryString - The QueryString method of passing values between web pages is one of the oldest methods of passing values between pages. A variable value is properly encoded before it is placed on a querystring. This is to make sure that characters that cause problems (*like symbols and spaces)* are encoded correctly. See the code below to see how QueryString functionality works.

```
//Code in InitialPage.aspx
String sString;
sString = Server.UrlEncode("string in InitialPage.aspx");
Response.Redirect("DestinationPage.aspx?Value=" & sString);

//Code in DestinationPage.aspx reads the QueryString
String sString;
sString = Request.QueryString("Value");
Response.Write("Your name is " & sString);
```

The data in the DestinationPage.aspx in the URL looks like this...

```
http://www.dotnetuncle.com/DestinationPage.aspx?Value=dotnetUncle
```

Context - The context object is used to send values between pages. It's similar to the session object, the difference being that, the Context object goes out of scope when the page is sent to a browser. Example code below shows how to use Context object.

```
'InitialPage.aspx stores value in context before sending it
Context.Items("MyData") = "dotnetuncle";
Server.Transfer("DestinationPage.aspx");
```

'DestinationPage.aspx retrieves the value from InitialPage.aspx's context
String sString;
sString = Context.Items("MyDate").ToString;
Response.Write("The data is as follows: " & sString);

Session - The session object is used to persist data across a user session during the user's visit to a website. It is almost same as the Context object. When we use Response.Redirect, it causes the Context object to go away, so rather the Session object is used in such a scenario. Session object uses more of server memory than a context object. Example code below shows how to use Session object.

'InitialPage.aspx stores value in session before sending it
Session.Items("MyData") = "dotnetuncle";
Response.Redirect("DestinationPage.aspx");

'DestinationPage.aspx retrieves the value from InitialPage.aspx's session
String sString;
sString = Session.Items("MyDate").ToString;
Response.Write("The data is as follows: " & sString);

You may notice above, I have used Response.Redirect with session object, and server.transfer with a context object.

Application, Cache, Session - objects are used to store global variables.

Q3. ★★What is the role of the ASP.NET worker process? What is aspnet_wp.exe?
A3. This question is hot in every interview. For faster execution of ASP.NET applications that are primarily based to be hosted on IIS servers, the **aspnet_wp.exe** comes into picture. This file *(aspnet_wp.exe)* is actually the ASP.NET worker process. The worker process is introduced to actually share the load on the IIS, so that application domains and other services may be maintained by a single worker process.

The aspnet_wp.exe worker process is a part of the Microsoft ASP.NET framework, and it is responsible for most of the technical processes in the ASP.NET framework. There may be multiple instances of ASP.NET worker process running on IIS 6 *(a process running as **inetinfo.exe**)*, depending on multiple application pools. The worker process handles all the requests passed to the ASP.NET framework, so you may say that it's actually the main engine that handles all requests pertaining to ASPNET. For example, when a request for an .aspx page is received by the IIS server, the dll called **aspnet_isapi.dll** passes this request to the aspnet_wp.exe worker process.

Q4. ★★Explain the page life cycle in ASP.NET 2.0
A4. **ASP.NET 2.0 Page Life Cycle** - The lifetime of an ASP.NET page is filled with events. A .NET technical interview might begin with this question. A series of processing steps takes place during this page life cycle. Following tasks are performed:

✓ Initialization

- ✓ Instantiation of controls
- ✓ Restoration & Maintenance of State
- ✓ Running Event Handlers
- ✓ Rendering of data to the browser

The life cycle may be broken down into **Stages** and **Events**. The stages reflect the broad spectrum of tasks performed. The following stages take place

1) **Page Request** - This is the first stage, before the page life cycle starts. Whenever a page is requested, ASP.NET detects whether the page is to be **requested, parsed and compiled** or whether the page can be **cached** from the system.

2) **Start** - In this stage, properties such as Request and Response are set. It's also determined at this stage whether the request is a new request or old, and thus it sets the **IsPostBack** property in the Start stage of the page life cycle.

3) **Page Initialization** - Each control of the page is assigned a unique identification ID. If there are themes, they are applied. Note that during the Page Initialization stage, neither postback data is loaded, nor any viewstate data is retrieved.

4) **Load** - If current request is a postback, then control values are retrieved from their viewstate.

5) **Validation** - The validate method of the validation controls is invoked. This sets the **IsValid** property of the validation control.

6) **PostBack Event Handling** - Event handlers are invoked, in case the request is a postback.

7) **Rendering** - Viewstate for the page is saved. Then **render** method for each control is called. A textwriter writes the output of the rendering stage to the output stream of the page's Response property.

8) **Unload** - This is the last stage in the page life cycle stages. It is invoked when the page is completely rendered. Page properties like **Response** and **Request** are unloaded.

> **Note**: Each stage has its own events within it. These events may be used by developers to handle their code.

Listed below are page events that are used frequently.

- ✓ **PreInit** - Checks the IsPostBack property. To create or recreate dynamic controls. To set master pages dynamically. Gets and Sets profile property values.
  Init - Raised after all controls are initialized, and skin properties are set.
  InitComplete - This event may be used, when we need to be sure that all initialization tasks are complete.
- ✓ **PreLoad** - If processing on a control or a page is required before the Load event.
- ✓ **Load** - invokes the OnLoad event on the page. The same is done for each child control on the page. May set properties of controls, create database connections.
- ✓ **Control Events** - These are the control specific events, such as button clicks, listbox item selections, etc.
- ✓ **LoadComplete** - To execute tasks that require that the complete page has been loaded.

- ✓ **PreRender** - Some methods are called before the PreRenderEvent takes place, like **EnsureChildControls**, data bound controls that have a dataSourceId set also call the **DataBind** method. Each control of the page has a PreRender event. Developers may use the prerender event to make final changes to the controls before it is rendered to the page.
- ✓ **SaveStateComplete** - ViewState is saved before this event occurs. However, if any change is made to the viewstate of a control then this is the event to be used. It cannot be used to make changes to other properties of a control.
- ✓ **Render** - This is a stage, not an event. The page object invokes this stage on each control of the page. This actually means that the ASP.NET server control's HTML markup is sent to the browser.
- ✓ **Unload** - This event occurs for each control. It takes care of cleanup activities such as wiping the database connections.

Q5. ★How and where to store global variables?

A5. Global variables **should always be used with caution**. They are the best means of storing data that has to be accessed anywhere. The most common ways of accessing global variables in ASP.NET are by using Application, Cache, and Session objects.

Application - Application objects are application level global variables that need to be shared for all user sessions. Thus, data specific to a user shouldn't be saved in application objects. While using application objects, the objects are **locked** so that multiple page requests cannot access a specific application object. Below is a code example that demonstrates the usage of the application object.

```
Application.Lock();
Application("UserData") = "dotnetuncle";
Application.UnLock();
Response.Redirect("DestinationPage.aspx");

//DestinationPage.aspx gets the value from the Application State
String sString = Application("UserData").ToString();
```

Cache - The cache object is similar to the application object in scope, however, it does not need any explicit locking and unlocking. The code below shows usage of Cache object:

```
Cache("Whiskyname") = "Blackdog";
Response.Redirect("DestinationPage.aspx");

//Destination.aspx retrieves the value from Cache object
String sString = Cache("Whiskyname").ToString();
```

The cache object also shares data across all user sessions. The cache object has features such as it can automatically expire cached content after specified time periods or once memory consumption has reached a maximum.

Session - The session object is used to store the data specific to a user for the entire length of a user's visit to a website. Below is a code that demonstrates the usage of the session object in ASP.NET:

```
//InitialPage.aspx stores the user's credentials in Session state
Session("UserName") = txtUserName.Text;
Server.Transfer("DestinationPage.aspx");

//DestinationPage.aspx gets the user's name from Session state
String sString = Session("UserName").ToString();
```

ASP.NET stores session values in the server memory. If there are plenty of active user's on a website, then the memory consumption on the server increases by leaps. Because of this reason, large websites use very less Session Variables. Session state can be configured to be automatically stored in a SQL Server database, or it can be configured to be stored centrally in a state server within a server farm. By default, a user's session ends 20 minutes after their last page request and their data goes out of scope, freeing it from memory. In case user information is to be tracked by a large website, then a cookie is preferred.

Cookie - A cookie is a piece of data that is stored on the user's browser. Thus, a cookie does not use any server memory.

Q6. How to store values between postbacks in ASP.NET? What is viewstate in ASP.NET?
A6. The postback question is the heart of any interview on ASP NET. When a postback happens *(i.e. when a form is submitted to a server)*, the variable values that are set in the code-behind page are erased from the memory of the client system. This concept would be different from what happens in Windows-based applications, where the variable persists in memory until they are freed from the memory either by the garbage collector, or by specific codes such as dispose or finalize.

In web applications, variable values simply get erased. But it is very simple to persist these values. They may be persisted using the V**iewstate** object. Before the postback is invoked, the variable's value is saved in a viewstate object. In the receiving page, the viewstate's value may be retrieved back. See example code below...

```
//Save the value in ViewState object before the PostBack
ViewState("SomeVar") = txtFirstName.text;

//Retrieve the value from ViewState object after the PostBack
String strFirstName = ViewState("SomeVar").ToString();
```

The viewstate value is saved and then passed to the next page by ASP.NET in the form of a **hidden variable**. Ideally, big values such as datasets should not be saved in a viewstate as they may tend to slow down the performance of the web page.

> **Note**: Apart from the viewstate object, values may also be sent across postbacks between pages using Application, Session and Cache objects.

Q7. ★What is a server control in ASP.NET?

A7. A server control in ASP.NET is a control that has the **runat="server"** attribute. The component is processed on the server, and its HTML equivalent stream is passed to the browser. Note that all server controls inherit from the **System.Web.UI.Control** class. The server side controls may be dragged to a web page from the standard toolbox. Note that HTML controls are not server side controls, but they may behave so if the runat="server" attribute is added to their source.

Q8. ★What is viewstate in ASP.NET?

A8. **Viewstate** object is used to persist data of variables across postbacks. It even existed in classic ASP. In ASP.NET, a variable's value is assigned to a viewstate object and then this is passed as a hidden variable and then may be retrieved by a page after a postback. See the example below...

```
//Save the value in ViewState object before the PostBack
ViewState("SomeVar") = txtFirstName.text;

//Retrieve the value from ViewState object after the PostBack
String strFirstName = ViewState("SomeVar").ToString();
```

Note that Viewstate object's value is **accessible only at page level**. This means that if a viewstate is created at page1.aspx, then it may be used only within page1.aspx after the postback, and cannot be used by any other page.

Q9. ★Which namespace does a webpage belong? What is the base class of a webpage?

A9. **System.Web.UI.Page** is the base class from which all web pages in ASP.NET derive from.

Q10. ★★How to store information about a user's locale in ASP.NET? What is localization?

A10. **Localization** is the feature of ASP.NET through which an application may be localized for a specific location. There are built-in mechanisms in .NET to allow localization process. The concept of localization is achieved in .NET as .NET is based on **Unicode**, thus it allows multiple characters of regions across the globe to be sent across in applications.

In .NET, the concept of localization is achieved using the **System.Globalization** namespace. A class named **CultureInfo** is used to localize .NET objects in the web applications. The functions provided in the globalization namespace work in tandem with the browser's culture encoding properties. In order to set the culture encoding of a web application, changes may simply be done in the **web.config** file.

```
<configuration>
 <system.web>
  <globalization
  requestencoding="utf-8"
  responseencoding=" utf-8"
  fileencoding=" utf-8"
```

```
  culture="hi-IN"
  uiculture="en" />
 </system.web>
</configuration>
```

Here, the default culture is set to Hindi *(hi-IN)*. However, the rest of the web application will use UTF8 character encoding. **The default UI culture is "en" by default.** Now in order to render different locality specific characters for different locations, different folders with their own Web.config files are created. Each of these folders will cater to a location. Note that in ASP.NET, a web.config file is allowed on any folder, this web.config file will override any settings provided in the web.config of any of its parent folder.

This is how locale specific directories are created for a site. Further note that culture settings may be set at page level as well. This is done using the **@Page directive** by setting its culture attribute to the desired culture.

```
<%@ Page Culture="hi-IN" UICulture="hi" ResponseEncoding="utf-8"%>
```

Instances of the CultureInfo class may also be created in the code, to set the culture of a page through code.

Q11. ★★How to add an event handler for a server control in ASP.NET?
A11. In an interview, it might be expected of you to write some code snippet as well.
Say we create a server control named btnSubmit. In order to add an event handler to it, see the code below:

Example (VB.NET):

```
Private Sub btnSubmit_Click() Handles btnSubmit.Click
btnSubmit.attribute.add("onclick","javascript:alert('You just added an attribute to the server button
control      btnSubmit by clicking on it');")
End Sub
```

Q12. ★What are validation controls in ASP.NET? How do validation controls work? What are validation groups in ASP.NET 2.0?
A12. An interview in ASP NET can't be really complete without preparing this question.
Validation controls in ASP.NET are server side controls that validate input values client-side. Sounds strange? Well, the best approach to validate any input value is to validate it client-side to avoid any postback and load to the server. This approach is followed to reduce the load on the server.

ASP.NET validation controls greatly improve the performance of a web application and may be used by web developers to reduce plenty of code that they used to write previously to validate input values using javascript or vbscript.

Input validations improvise security of a web application, by preventing SQL Injection attacks.

There are 6 validations controls in both ASP.NET 1.1 and ASP.NET 2.0

1) **RequiredFieldValidator** - as the name suggests, this control makes sure that the input box is not left blank.
2) **CompareValidator** - This control validates values in two controls, and checks for equality
3) **RangeValidator** - This validation control makes sure that the value entered in the control falls within a range specified. This specification may be done using its properties.
4) **RegularExpression** - Based on a regular expression, values entered in an input box must match the ones specified by this control's RegularExpression property
5) **CustomValidator** - This type of validator control may be customized & created by a developer as per need
6) **ValidationSummary** - This control may be used to show the summary of the information gathered using rest of the other validation controls

To use a validation control, set a validation control on a form. Associate it with a server control by using its **ControlToValidate** property. Note that the server control has a property called **CausesValidation** and this is set to **true** for the validation control to trigger. This property is true by default for every server control. The validation control also has an **ErrorMessage** property that is assigned some text to explain what the error is, in case the validation control is triggered. The validation control actually calls a client-side script that comes with ASP.NET, and this script does the job of validation for us. All this validation is done client-side.

Suppose we want to use the RequiredFieldValidator control so that a textbox isn't left blank, for this, see the inline code below:

```
<asp:Button ID="btnGo" runat="server" Text="Go" />
<asp:TextBox ID="txtSomeText" runat="server" Text="" CausesValidation="true"></asp:TextBox>
<asp:RequiredFieldValidator ID="rfvTextbox" runat="server" ControlToValidate="txtSomeText"
ErrorMessage="Please Enter Some Text" ></asp:RequiredFieldValidator>
```

Tip: The Page.IsValid property of the page is **true** only if there is no validation error returned.

Validation controls are supported by Internet Explorer, Firefox and Opera.

ASP.NET 2.0 provides a method to allow multiple sets of controls that may be grouped together into a validation group. The purpose of this approach makes it easy to invoke validation checks on specific server controls and not all of them who have an associated validation control.

Q13. ★What is global.asax in ASP.NET? Application_start, Session_start?
A13. The global.asax file is used to add application level logic & processing. Note that the global.asax does not handle any UI related processing, nor does it process individual page level requests. It basically controls the following events:

✓ Application_Start
✓ Application_End
✓ Session_Start
✓ Session_End

Visual Studio 2003 automatically creates this file for every web application, but in Visual Studio 2005, this file has to be added to the web project separately, same is the case with VS 2008.

Code in the global.asax is compiled when the web application is built for the first time. The application level code and variables may be declared in Application_Start. Similarly, session level code & variables may be declared in Session_Start event. Application level events are for the entire application, and may be used for any user, while Session level events are user specific for a length of a session.

Q14. ★★★What is an HTTP handler in ASP.NET? Can we use it to upload files? What is HttpModule?

A14. The **HttpHandler** and **HttpModule** is used by ASP.NET to handle requests. Whenever the IIS Server receives a request, it looks for an ISAPI filter that is capable of handling web requests. In ASP.NET, this is done by **aspnet_isapi.dll**. Same kind of process happens when an ASP .NET page is triggered. It looks for HttpHandler in the web.config files for any request setting. As in machine.config default setting, the .aspx files are mapped to PageHandlerFactory, and the .asmx files are mapped to the WebServiceHandlerFactory. There are many requests processed by ASP.NET in this cycle, such as **BeginRequest, AuthenticateRequest, AuthorizeRequest, AcquireRequestState, ResolveRequestCache, Page Constructor, PreRequestHandlerExecute, Page.Init, Page.Load, PostRequestHandlerExecute, ReleaseRequestState, UpdateRequestCache, EndRequest, PreSendRequestHeaders, and PreSendRequestContent.**

Yes, the HttpHandler may be used to upload files.

HttpModules are components of .NET that implement the System.Web.IHttpModule interface. These components register for some events and are then invoked during the request processing. It implements the Init and the Dispose methods. HttpModules has events like **AcquireRequestState, AuthenticateRequest, AuthorizeRequest, BeginRequest, Disposed , EndRequest, Error, PostRequestHandlerExecute, PreRequestHandlerExecute, PreSendRequestHeaders, ReleaseRequestState, ResolveRequestCache, UpdateRequestCache**

Q15. ★What is a session in ASP.NET? What are the different ways to maintain session?

A15. The most common used object, due to its usefulness is the Session object, and hence, it is a must-know in any interview related to ASP.NET or web based programming.

Session - The session object is used to store the data specific to a user for the entire length of a user's visit to a website. Below is a code that shows usage of the session object in ASP.NET...

```
//InitialPage.aspx stores the user's credentials in Session state
Session("UserName") = txtUserName.Text;
Server.Transfer("DestinationPage.aspx");
```

```
//DestinationPage.aspx gets the user's name from Session state
String sString = Session("UserName").ToString();
```

Q16. ★What is a cookie? What are the limitations of cookie? What is a permanent cookie?

A16. The cookie object is the essence of any interview, be it ASP NET interview or Java interview or PHP interview.

Cookie - A cookie is a piece of data that is stored on a user's browser. Thus, a cookie does not use any server memory. It is actually a small text file which is created by the browser on the hard disk of the user. It is actually a piece of information in the form of text strings. A web server sends a cookie to a user (client browser) and then the browser stores it.

A cookie is used to store information of a user & information about a user's preferences.

How does a cookie work? - When a user visits a site, says www.dontboozeanddrive.com, and creates a profile out there, the server sends an ID *(basically an ID to track this user)* and saves the ID through the user's browser in the form of a cookie on the user's system. When the user revisits this site, the website tracks the user's system for the existence of any cookie, and in case it finds a cookie, it customizes the site based on the user's settings and preferences.

Now let's talk about how to create a cookie in ASP.NET. It is pretty simple. There is a class in the **System.Web** namespace by the name **HttpCookie**. This class may be used to easily create a cookie on the user's system. Below is a code sample on how to use a cookie in ASP.NET:

```
//Creating a cookie HttpCookie sampleCookie = new HttpCookie("UserColorSetting");
sampleCookie.Values.Add("Background", txtBackgroundColor.Text);
sampleCookie.Expires = #12/31/2010#; Response.Cookies.Add(sampleCookie);
```

```
//Getting a cookie value from the user's computer
String sGetCookie;
sGetCookie = Request.Cookies("UserColorSetting")("Background").ToString();
```

Limitation of Cookies - Cookies are meant for infrequent storage of small pieces of information. They are not meant as a normal communication or mechanism. Note that web browsers are not required to save more than 300 cookies total, nor more than 20 cookies per web server (for the entire server, not just for the page or site on the server), nor to retain more than 4 kilobytes of data per cookie *(both name and value count towards this 4 kilobyte limit)*. The biggest limitation of these is the 20 cookies per server limit, and so it is not a good idea to use a different cookie for each variable that has to be saved. Rather save a single cookie containing a lot of information.

Q17. ★How to set the view state for a server control? What is the Enableviewstate property?

A17. This is a popular interview question. The **enableviewstate** property of a server control indicates whether the server control persists its viewstate. It also controls the viewstate behavior of the child controls within it.

So what is Viewstate? - Viewstate is the property of a server control that groups all the other property values of the control, so that the entire set of property values is preserved across multiple HTTP requests. The **enableviewstate** property when set to true, makes the viewstate property persist all the other property values.

How does viewstate work? - The viewstate values are passed as an HTML hidden input element when HTTP requests are invoked. To see how a viewstate variable's value looks like, right click any aspx page and click view source, you will find something like this...

```
type="hidden" name="__VIEWSTATE" id="__VIEWSTATE" value="/wEPDwULLTEw.. .. .. ..
2FzcF9hc3AubmV0LmFzcHgfB=="
```

An instance of the **StateBag** class is created to store the property values.

There are scenarios when a Viewstate is set to false. For example, say a database request is loaded to a server control, then the size of the database values may be humongous, for which the Viewstate is set to false.

Example below shows how the viewstate is set to work:

```
<asp:Textbox id="txtName" runat="server" text="" enableviewstate="true" >
```

Q18. ★What is smart navigation?
A18. Before explaining what smart navigation is, let me point out that Smart Navigation is obsolete in .NET 2.0. It works with 1.1 & versions before it. The SetFocus and MaintainScrollPositionOnPostBack are used instead

Smart Navigation basically enhances a web pages' performance by doing the following:

- ✓ It eliminates the flash caused during navigation
- ✓ It persists element focus during postbacks
- ✓ It persists scroll position during postbacks between pages
- ✓ It retains the lasts page information in the history of the browser
- ✓ It is suggested not to use SmartNavigation because it does not work with many browsers.

Q19. ★★ What is the difference between a web farm and web garden in ASP.NET?
A19. An ASP.NET interview can't be really complete without the web farm question.

So what is a web farm? A **Web Farm** is a setup of a website across multiple servers.

A **Web Garden** is a setup of a website on a single server with multiple processors.

Q20. ★★Can a dataset be stored in a viewstate?

A20. This can be a tricky question in interviews. Yes, a dataset may be stored in a viewstate. However, a viewstate is passed to the server as a hidden variable. Precaution should be taken that the dataset size is not too big, otherwise such an activity will take a toll on both the client and server system resources, and ultimately slow down rendering of the data on the client system. Also note that the viewstate data may not be sent to another aspx page, as that's a limitation of a viewstate object.

Q21. ★What is the purpose of @Register directive in ASP.NET? How to create Web User Controls in ASP.NET?

A21.Good developers must know the Register and User Control concept before any interview in ASP.NET.

Directives in ASP.NET are used to set attributes for a page. The **@Register** directive is a directive used to register user defined controls on a web page. A user created server control has an **ascx** extension. These controls inherit from the namespace **System.Web.UI.UserControl**. This namespace inherits from the **System.Web.UI.Control**.

A user control may be embedded in an **aspx** web page using the @Register directive. A user control cannot be executed on its own independently, but may be registered on a web page and then used out there. Below is the syntax for registering a @register directive in an aspx page in ASP.NET

```
<%@ Register TagPrefix="UC1" TagName="UserControl1" Src="UserControl1.ascx" %>
```

The **TagPrefix** attributes is used to specify a unique namespace for the user control. The **TagName** is a name used to refer a user control uniquely by its name. Say we want to use this control in a webpage; we may use the code below...

```
<UC1:UserControl1 runat="server"/>
```

CHAPTER 5 – ASP.NET 2.0

Q1. ★Can we bind data to a server control without writing code in .NET?
A1. Yes, that is possible. ASP.NET 2.0 has the feature of declarative solution for data binding which requires no code at all for the most common data scenarios, such as:

- ✓ Selecting and displaying
- ✓ Data Sorting
- ✓ Paging and Caching
- ✓ Data Updating
- ✓ Inserting and Deleting Data

Q2. ★How to use Masterpages and Contentpages in ASP.NET 2.0? What is a ContentPage? How to setup master-content pages in ASP.NET 2.0?
A2. A Master page is the mother of the page and the content page is the baby! There may be many babies of the mother. A master page may have plenty of content pages within it. There also may be a master page within a master page, which is called a nested master page. Now common, that doesn't mean two mothers!

So what's a master page in ASP.NET 2.0? A Master Page is a page that contains markup and controls that are shared across multiple pages in your site. For example, if required that all pages should have the same header and footer banners or the common navigation menu, the Master page can be written once, and all the content pages can access the common master page. The content pages inherit the tags inside the master page.

How to define a master page?

Well, to define a Master Page, it may be written like a normal page. Master Pages can contain markup, controls, or code, or any combination of these tags. The **Content** pages are rendered in a master page control called as **ContentPlaceHolder control**. A ContentPlaceHolder defines a region of the master page rendering that can be exchanged with content from a page associated to the master. A ContentPlaceHolder can also contain default content, when in case the derive page does not need to override this content. Below is the markup of how to use a **Contentplaceholder**.

```
<asp:contentplaceholder id="ContentPlaceHolderInterviewQuestions" runat="server"/>
```

```
<asp:contentplaceholder id="ContentPlaceHolderInterviewQuestions" runat="server">
<h3>Welcome to the .NET Interview Questions website!</h3>
</asp:contentplaceholder>
```

A master page has the extension **.master**, unlike a normal web form that has the extension .aspx. A page may derive from a Master Page by defining a MasterPageFile attribute on its Page directive. Below is the markup of a content page.

```
<%@ Page MasterPageFile="Masterpage.master" %>
<asp:content id="Content1" contentplaceholderid="ContentPlaceHolderInterviewQuestions"
runat="server">
Here goes contents of ContentPlaceHolderInterviewQuestions </asp:content>
</asp:content>
```

So how does a content page access a master page? It is also possible for a Content Page to programmatically access a Master Page. A ContentPage may create a strongly-typed reference to the Master Page using the <%@ MasterType %> directive, which specifies the virtual path to the masterpage as below:

```
<%@ MasterType VirtualPath="Masterpage.master" %>
```

The Content Page may then reference the Master Page using the **Master property** of the Page class:

```
Label lb1 = Master.FindControl("label2");
```

As in the example above, FooterText is a public property exposed on the Master Page, whereas label2 is a server side control on the Master Page.

> **Note**: The **FindControl** method is a very useful and a very important method, that may be used for finding a control in a content page from a master page and vice versa.

Q3. ★What is a nested Masterpage in ASP.NET 2.0? Can there be a master page inside a masterpage?
A3. When a master page is placed inside the contentplaceholder of a masterpage, then the masterpage **is said to be nested**. In other words, there is one parent masterpage, and the child masterpage is inside the contentplaceholder of the parent masterpage. Yes, we can have multiple numbers of Master pages in an ASP.NET 2.0 web application.

Q4. ★What is a SiteMapPath control in ASP.NET 2.0?
A4. A **SiteMapPath** control is a Navigation Control that comes along with the ASP.NET 2.0 framework. The SiteMapPath control consists of site link's data in XML format. The emergence of the SiteMapPath control in ASP.NET 2.0 has totally eliminated the clumsy code used in bread crumbs by veteran web developers in Classic ASP and ASP.NET 1.1. These bread crumbs were comparatively tougher to maintain.

Now say you need to maintain a Sitemap of a Site having the following links.
Example: Home Products   Medicines   Soaps   Alcohol Support   Phone Support Email Support Contact Us

Instead of hard coding these links inside your code, all this information may be maintained in an XML based Web.sitemap file which can be bind to an asp:SiteMapPath control, and this would display like a website breadcrumb. Quite easier than before!

The SiteMapPath control's SiteMapProvider property is used to set the site's sitemap provider. The sitemap provider is another control called **XmlDataSource** control. This needs to be registered in the web.config file. If the SiteMapProvider property is not specified, then the default SiteMap Provider information is picked up from the web.config file.

Note: The other two navigation controls in ASP.NET 2 are the Menu control and the TreeView control.

The XmlDataSource control loads an XML file that is specified using the **DataFile** property. This control inherits from the **HierarchicalDataSourceControl** class.

Example XML below:
```
<asp:SiteMapPath ID="smm1" runat="server" SiteMapProvider="xds1"></asp:SiteMapPath>
<asp:XmlDataSource ID="xds1" DataFile="somefile.xml" runat="server"></asp:XmlDataSource>
```

If DataFile is not used in the XmlDataSource, the siteMapFile property can be set in the web.config.
In order to specify XML Data Source in the web.config file, refer the code below:

```
<configuration>
<system.web>

<siteMap defaultProvider="XmlSiteMapProvider" enabled="true">
 <providers>
 <clear/>
 <add name="XmlSiteMapProvider"
 <description="Default SiteMap provider"
 <type="System.Web.XmlSiteMapProvider"
 <siteMapFile="~/Web.sitemap"
 </>
 </providers>
</siteMap>
</system.web>
</configuration>
```

Q5. ★★How to sort the contents of a GridView control?
A5. The ASP.NET 2.0 GridView control is a powerful control that enables sorting of the rows based on a column, all this is possible, without writing code.

The GridView control relies on the underlying data source control to which this is bound for the sorting capability. The GridView needs to have an **AccessDataSource** or a **SQlDataSource** or an ObjectDataSource.

The **AllowSorting** property of the GridView control, when set to **true**, enables sorting of the GridView. A sortable GridView has the Header column represented as a LinkButton control. When this Link Button is clicked, the **Sorting** event of the GridView is raised server-side, which causes a postback and in turn, sorts the GridView control's records.

Q6. ★★What does the Hotspot class in .NET do? What is an ImageMap in ASP.NET?

A6. An **ImageMap** is an ASP.NET control that allows clicks inside a polygon like (called **Hotspot**) region in a webpage. Well, that actually means you may create a star-shaped or diamond shaped button. Wow!

There are several pre-defined shapes allowed inside an ImageMap for which templates may be used. For example, for a rectangle, an **asp:RectangularHotSpot** may be used. For a circle, an **asp:CircleHotSpot** may be used. For creating stars & diamonds, an **asp:PolygonHotSpot** may be used. An image may also be put in an ImageMap which may be specified by its ImageUrl property.

In order to invoke an event, the **HotSpotMode** property needs to be set to PostBack. Further, if several HotSpots are placed inside an ImageMap, the event of the ImageMap may be passed a value using the **PostBackValue** property.

The code example below shows how to create a Polygon HotSpot using an ImageMap.

```
<asp:ImageMap ID="ImageMap1" Runat="Server"
ImageUrl="Photo.gif" OnClick="SomeEvent"
AlternateText="Click Here"
HotSpotMode="Navigate">

<asp:PolygonHotSpot
AlternateText="Click Here Too!"
Coordinates="100,150, 250,350, 210,290, 90,350, 60,240"
NavigateUrl="http://www.asp.net"
Target="_blank"/>
</asp:ImageMap>
```

Q7. ★★How do we update and delete data in a GridView? Explain the Datakeynames property in .NET?
A7. The best way to Update or Delete a record in a GridView control is to include a CheckBox column and a Submit Button.

The GridView has its own Delete and Edit functionality. If the GridView is populated with data using a SqlDataSource, check out the wizard that comes along with the SqlDataSource. It may be used to automatically create an SQL Delete command and specify the delete parameters. The **DataKeyNames** property of the GridView is set to a field name of the Table.

Q8. ★★Describe the security authentication process in ASP.NET?
A8. When a user requests a web page, there exists a process of security, so that every anonymous user is checked for authentication before gaining access to the webpage. The following points are followed in the sequence for authentication when a client attempts a page request:

✓ A .aspx web page residing on an IIS web server is requested by an end user
✓ IIS checks for the user's credentials
✓ Authentication is done by IIS. If authenticated, a token is passed to the ASP.NET worker process along with the request

✓ Based on the authentication token from IIS, and on the web.config settings for the requested resource, ASP.NET impersonates the end user to the request thread.

For impersonation, the web.config **impersonate** attribute's value is checked.

Q9. ★Tell something about the Website Administrative Tool in ASP.NET 2.0?
A9. In Visual Studio, the development IDE provides an interface for editing the web.config rather than manually editing the web.config.

In the IDE, click on "Website" and then on "ASP.NET Configuration". This shall open the Website configuration tool. Note that the Web Site Administration Tool is a set of prebuilt ASP.NET 2.0 web pages and resources that are located within the C:\Inetpub\wwwroot\aspnet_webadmin\2_0_40607 directory.

Q10. ★What is Authentication? What are the different types of Authentication?
A10. In a client-server environment, there are plenty of cases where the server has to interact and identify the client that sends a request to the server. **Authentication** is the process of determining and confirming the identity of the client.

Note: If a client is not successfully identified, it is said to be anonymous.

Types of Authentication

✓ Windows Authentication
✓ Forms Authentication
✓ Passport Authentication *(This is not much used much nowadays)*

The Windows Authentication and Forms Authentication are the famous ones, as Passport Authentication is related to a few websites (such as microsoft.com, hotmail.com, msn.com etc. only).

Windows Authentication is implemented mostly in Intranet scenarios. When a browser (client) sends a **Request** to a server where in windows authentication has been implemented, the initial request is anonymous in nature. The server sends back a **Response** with a message in HTTP Header. This Prompts a Window to display a Modal Dialog Box on the browser, where the end user may enter the "User name" and "Password".

The end user enters the credentials, which are then validated against the User Store on the Windows server. Note that each user who access the Web Application in a Windows Authentication environment needs to have a Windows Account in the company network.

How to avoid or disable the modal dialog box in a Windows Authentication environment?

By enabling the Windows Integrated Authentication checkbox for the web application through settings in IIS, the modal dialog box for Windows Authentication will go away.

Forms Authentication is used in Internet based scenarios, where it's not practical to provide a Windows based account to each and every user to the Web Server. In a Forms Authentication environment, the user enters credentials, usually a User Name and a corresponding Password, which is validated against a User Information Store, ideally a database table.

Forms Authentication Ticket is the cookie stored on the user's computer, when a user is authenticated. This helps in automatically logging in a user when he/she re-visits the website. When a Forms Authentication ticket is created, when a user re-visits a website, the Forms Authentication Ticket information is sent to the Web Server along with the HTTP Request.

Q11. ★What is Authorization in ASP.NET?
A11. **Authorization** in simple words means "which user can access which resource on a website". **Authorization** of users may be set in the web.config file. See web.config snippet below:

```
<authorization>
   <deny users="?" /> <!-- Allow all users -->
   <!-- <allow users="[user list separated by commas]"
   roles="[role list separated by commas]"/>
   <deny users="[user list separated by commas]"
   roles="[role list separated by commas]"/>
   -->
</authorization>
```

Based on the user and the role, access to different folders across the website may be controlled using the authorization feature of ASP.NET

Q12. ★★★What is IIS Metabase? How to edit IIS Metabase? How to backup IIS Metabase file?
A12. **IIS Metabase** - sounds like geek stuff right! What is IIS Metabase??? In the simple words, IIS Metabase is the repository of the configuration values that are set in the **internet Information Server** *(IIS)*. The IIS Metabase in an XML file. It may be controlled through program or manually too.

In order to edit IIS Metabase entries, the user needs to have administrative rights on the system. To do this, in the run window, type "**inetmgr**". Browse to "Local Computer" and right click it. Click on "Properties". Select the "Enable Direct Metabase Edit" check box.

Many times, due to the presence of multiple versions of .NET framework, some settings in the IIS Metabase may get affected and cause your program not to run. For such scenarios, you may take a backup of the IIS Metabase XML file and recover it. To create a portable backup, open run window and type "inetmgr". Next browse to "Local Computer" and go to "All Tasks". Next, click on

Backup/Restore Configuration. Next, click on "Create Backup". In the textbox for Configuration Backup name, type a name for your backup file. Also, select the encrypt backup option and then type a password. To finish the process, click "OK".

Search for **Metabase.xml** file on your IIS Web Server.

Q13. ★★★What is mixed mode authentication in ASP.NET?
A13. **Mixed mode authentication** in an asp.net web application has the ability to feature both Forms Authentication and Windows Authentication to the end user.

In such a web application, the website user is identified based on whether the user is accessing the site from within the local domain or an external domain. When the user is from within the domain, Windows Authentication is applied and thus, the user can be configured to have higher authorization rights. The users logging into the web application from an external domain access the site using Forms authentication.

But this is tricky!!! For such an application to work there needs to be two virtual directories setup for the web application on the IIS. This is because an asp.net web application cannot be set to two different authentication modes. So if someone asks whether an ASP.NET application support 2 authentication modes at the same time??? The answer is **TECHNICALLY NO! But there is a workaround!!!**

The windows authentication site's authentication is basically used to get information about the intranet users and this is passed to the web application for Forms authentication. In such a scenario, the windows authentication information from the windows authentication site in IIS is passed to the Forms Authentication and thus user role is verified.

Q14. ★★What is Provider Model and Personalization in ASP.NET 2.0?
A14. The Provider model in ASP.NET 2.0 is based on the Provider Design Pattern that was created in the year 2002 and later implemented in the .NET Framework 2.0. The Provider Model supports automatic creation of users and their respective roles by creating entries of them directly in the SQL Server *(May even use MS Access and other custom data sources)*. This model also supports automatically creating the user table's schema.

The Provider model has two security providers in it: **Membership provider and Role Provider**. The membership provider saves inside it the user name (id) and corresponding passwords, whereas the Role provider stores the Roles of the users.

For SQL Server, the **SqlMembershipProvider** is used, while for MS Access, the **AccessMembershipProvider** is used. The Security settings may be set using the website administration tool. Automatically, the AccessMembershipProvider creates a Microsoft Access Database file named aspnetdb.mdb inside the application's **App_Data** folder.

ASP.NET 2.0 Personalization - Personalization allows information about visitors to be persisted on a data store so that the information can be useful to the visitor when they visit the site again. In ASP.NET 2.0, this is controlled by a Personalization API. Before the Personalization Model came into existence, the prior versions of ASP.NET used of the old **Session** object to take care of re-visits. Now comes the **Profile object**.

In order to use a Profile object, some settings need to be done in web.config. The example below shall explain how to use a profile object:

```
//Add this to the System.Web in web.config

<profile>
<properties>
 <add name="FirstName" type="System.String"/>
 <add name="LastName" type="System.String"/>
</properties>
</profile>

'In Page_Load event, add the following...

If Profile.FirstName <> "" Then
  Panel1.Visible = False
  Response.Write("Welcome Back Dear :, " & Profile.FirstName & ", " & Profile.LastName)
Else
  Panel1.Visible = True
End If
```

Here is the code how to save the profile properties in an event to save it.

```
Profile.FirstName = txtFirstName.Text
Profile.LastName = txtLastName.Text
```

CHAPTER 6 – ASP.NET 3.5

Q1. ★What is new in the ASP.NET 3.5 Framework?
A1. The ASP.NET 3.5 framework is packed with a stream of new controls. It's an extension to the existing set of controls that comes with the ASP.NET 2.0 framework. This implies that if you are working on Visual Studio 2005 and .NET 2.0, simply download the ASP.NET 3.5 framework from the Microsoft website. You will need minor changes in the site settings in IIS during site deployment, by changing the version of .NET. In case you are using Visual Studio 2008, it comes along with the .NET 3.5 Framework, so you need not worry about the extra effort of downloading .NET 3.5. In short, .NET Framework 3.5 goes best with Visual Studio 2008.

Whilst working with Visual Studio 2008, the web.config is always added by default, while creating a new web application, unlike what we witness with Visual Studio 2005.

Q2. ★How does a datapager control work?
A2. Controls such as the GridView and the Repeater exhibit the pagination behavior. This is useful when display results return far too many records than an ideal web page height. A search may return countless records, but the web page size should not ideally go on and on depending on the number of records returned. For this, the **Page Number** or the **Previous-Next** feature appears at the bottom of the display results seem to be more ideal. For this purpose, the DataPager control has been introduced.

> While using a ListView control, a DataPager control may be used along with it, to provide a paging functionality. The DataPager has a property called **PagerControlId** which is set to the ID of the ListView control.

Q3. ★What is the ListView control?
A3. The ListView control is like an advanced Repeater control, and is as good as a GridView control in terms of features it has. It may be set to any standard data source such as SQL, Oracle, Access, XML and even LINQ.

Say you want to display a matrix of values with three records per row, the ListView control is the ideal solution. The ListView settings may be made manually using the aspx page, or may also be set using the Smart Tag feature to launch the properties dialog box.

Q4. ★What is a ScriptManager?
A4. Every Ajax enabled page in ASP.NET that makes use of the Ajax Library needs to have a boss or a manager that takes care of the internal Ajaxification process. All this is controlled by the ScriptManager control. **Every page should have not more than one ScriptManager control**. It takes care of the Javascript functionalities and the partial postbacks made by the web page by taking care of the **XmlHttpRequest** object from behind the scenes.

The ScriptManager is a class as well as a control. This was introduced in ASP.NET 3.5, before which it had to be used in ASP.NET 2.0 through the Ajax Library for .NET.

If the **EnablePartialPostback** property of the ScriptManager is set to false, the web page exhibits a full page postback.

In the aspx code, the ScriptManager control acts as the bucket for the UpdatePanel control.

Q5. ★★What is the role of the ScriptManagerProxy control?
A5. There might be a scenario when your masterpage and content page need to have separate ScriptManager controls. For such situations, the **ScriptManagerProxy** control comes to rescue. Here, the masterpage may contain the ScriptManager control, and the content page may use the ScriptManagerProxy control. However, internally, the ScripManagerProxy control communicates with the corresponding ScriptManager class of the web page. The ScriptManagerProxy control actually transfers its set of responsibilities to the ScriptManager control.

Q6. ★What is an UpdatePanel control?
A6. This is the control that wraps all the controls that need to be partially posted back. A web page may comprise of several UpdatePanels. In case there is any event happening within the controls wrapped inside an UpdatePanel control, the entire page isn't posted back, rather only the contents within the UpdatePanel are posted back to the web server. If the partial postback has to be avoided, set the **ChildrenAsTriggers** property of the UpdatePanel to false.

Further, the Triggers of an UpdatePanel may be used to set the application in such a way that the partial postback of the UpdatePanel may be invoked from controls that lie outside the UpdatePanel.

Q7. ★What is an UpdateProgress control?
A7. There are scenarios where a request may take time, an image may take time to load, business logic may a lot of time to calculate, and data may take time to load due to diversities in the source. In UpdatePanels, because postbacks are partial in nature, the browser's default progress bar does not appear. For avoiding any confusion to the end user that a page process is going on in the background the UpdateProgress control may be used. This is like a progress bar that appears to the end user, signifying that a process is going on. Usually, the image is a moving .gif file.

Q8. ★What is LINQ?
A8. **LINQ** *(Language Integrated Query)* empowers .NET developers with a native data querying platform. It is accompanied with a query language. LINQ is a part of .NET 3.5 (and above). LINQ defines operators that permit developers to code queries in a consistent fashion over databases, XML & objects. A control called as the LinqDataSource control allows to use LINQ to filter, group and order data before binding to the List controls.

Q9. ★★Tell something about the ASP.NET merge tool.
A9. ASP.NET 3.5 adds a new merge tool which is the **aspnet_merge.exe** tool. This tool allows merging and managing assemblies created by the **aspnet_compiler.exe**. As such, this tool was available before .NET 3.5 was launched, but as an add-on.

Q10. ★★Which new assemblies were added in .NET 3.5?
A10. The following are some of the key assemblies added in .NET 3.5:

- ✓ **System.Data.Linq.dll** - This has the implementation for LINQ to SQL
- ✓ **System.Core.dll** – This includes the implementation for LINQ to Objects
- ✓ **System.Xml.Linq.dll** - This assembly has the implementation for LINQ to XML
- ✓ **System. .DataSetExtensions.dll** - This has implementation for LINQ to DataSet
- ✓ **System.Web.Extensions.dll** - This assembly has the implementation for ASP.NET AJAX (new enhancements added) and new web controls as explained earlier

Q11. ★Can an application built on .NET Framework 2.0 be opened and run in Visual Studio 2008?
A11. Yes. In fact, it can also run in Visual Studio 2010.

Q12. ★Can multiple versions of ASP.NET be installed on the same machine?
A12. Yes.

CHAPTER 7 – ASP.NET 4.0

Q1. ★What is new in ASP.NET 4.0?
A1. ASP.NET 4.0 introduces a number of new features such as:

1. Web.config refactoring
2. Extensible Output Caching
3. Auto-start Web Applications
4. Permanent Redirection
5. Shrinking Session State
6. Expanding the range of allowable URLs
7. Expanding the range of blocked URL characters
8. Performance monitoring for a single application in a single worker process
9. Setting meta tags with Page.meta keywords
10. Enabling ViewState for individual controls
11. Built-in routing with Web Forms
12. Readable control IDs through ClientIDMode
13. ASP.NET Chart Control (this was earlier an add-on)
14. HTML encoded code expressions

Q2. ★What is Web.config refactoring?
A2. Most of the entities in the web.config have been moved to the machine.config file. This is how the new web.config looks like:

```
<?xml version="1.0"?> <configuration>
  <system.web>
   <compilation targetFramework="4.0" />
  </system.web>
</configuration>
```

The refactoring allows moving the common references in the Web.config file to be stored on a system level location, rather than an application level location. Such an approach reduces the heavy size of the Web.config file, which otherwise had to be processed in its entirety all the time the application ran. Further, this allows developers to specify which version of the .NET Framework has to be used for the execution of the web application.

Q3. ★★What is the benefit of Extensible Output Caching in ASP.NET 4.0?
A3. Cache object is stored on the Web Server. Extensible Output Caching empowers you to store your cache objects on other machines such as other local disks, remote disks and cloud storage locations.

Benefit: You can now decide what to be cached on your busy Web Server, and what to cache on other locations.

How to do it?
1. Create a class that derives from the new System.**Web.Caching.OutputCacheProvider**
2. Set the following in the web.config file, under the new providers sub section:

```
<caching>
        <outputCache defaultProvider="AspNetInternalProvider">
```

```
    <providers> <add name="DiskCache"
type="Test.OutputCacheEx.DiskOutputCacheProvider, DiskCacheProvider"/>      </providers>
    </outputCache>
</caching>
```

3. Set the following for the control:

```
<%@ OutputCache Duration="60" VaryByParam="None" providerName="DiskCache" %>
```

4. Set the following per request:
This is to be added in **global.asax**

```
public override string GetOutputCacheProviderName(HttpContext context)
{
  if (context.Request.Path.EndsWith("Advanced.aspx"))
    return "DiskCache";
  else
    return base.GetOutputCacheProviderName(context);
}
```

Extensible Output Caching allows to intelligently identifying which components of a web page should be cached. For example, you can decide to cache the top five pages of your website.

Q4. ★★Can ASP.NET applications continue running even if IIS is reset in ASP.NET 4.0?
A4. Yes, this is possible in applications built on top of ASP.NET 4.0 *(and onwards)*. Historically, ASP.NET applications take time to load at the first time a request is passed to the web server.

Pre-Requisites: IIS 7.5+, Windows Server 2008 R2

Advantage

Web application keeps running when **IISRESET** is run. For this, you need to set the IIS Application Pool as **AlwaysRunning**. When the new IIS Worker Process is up, the new changes start reflecting. This effectively means that there would be **NO INTERRUPTION.**

In the file **applicationHost.config**

```
<applicationpools>
<add name="MyApplicationPool" startMode="AlwaysRunning" />
</applicationpools>
```

Next, you can specify which applications need to be pre-started, when IIS is setup:

```
<sites>
 <site name="MySite" id="1">
      <application path="/" serviceAutoStartEnabled="true"
serviceAutoStartProvider="PrewarmMyCache" />
 </site>
 </sites>
```

Q5. ★What is the advantage of the Response.RedirectPermanent() method in ASP.NET 4.0?
A5. When a web page has moved permanently, it is recommended to use the Response.RedirectPermanent method in ASP.NET 4.0.

Example (C#):

RedirectPermanent("/newpath/foroldcontent.aspx");

The advantage is that the search engines will take this a permanent redirection *(Status 301)* and will remove old page from its cache/database, and include new page for better performance on search.

Q6. ★★Compare Response.Redirect(), Response.RedirectPermanent() and Server.Transfer().
A6. The points below explain each one of these methods:

- ✓ **Response.Redirect()** - Search Engine will take this redirection as Temporary(Status 302) and always keep the old page in its cache.
- ✓ **Response.RedirectPermanent()** - Search Engine will take this a permanent redirection(Status 301) and will remove the old page from its cache/database and include new page for better performance on search.
- ✓ **Server.Transfer()** - Search Engine will be unaware of any redirection that took place (Status 200) and will keep old page in its cache/database. It will think that the old page is producing the output response of the new page.

Q7. ★★Explain the concept of shrinking session state in ASP.NET 4.0?
A7. The ASP.NET 4.0 Framework has a mechanism to compress session objects that are set through the 'out of proc' mechanism. We are aware of two types of Out of Proc mechanisms to persist session data namely SQLServer and StateServer. What you need to remember is the new property:

compressionEnabled="true"

This makes it sure that the session object is compressed before it is persisted, thereby saving memory and improving performance. The Session object is serialized before it is sent to the remote location.

ASP.NET 4.0, compress (and decompress) serialized session state by using the .NET Framework **System.IO.Compression.GZipStream** class.

Q8. ★★How do you expand the size of allowable URL size in ASP.NET 4.0?
A8. Read on:

<httpRuntime maxRequestPathLength="260" maxQueryStringLength="2048" />

To allow longer or shorter paths *(the portion of the URL that does not include the protocol, server name, and the query string)*, modify the **maxRequestPathLength** attribute. To allow longer or shorter query strings, modify the value of the **maxQueryStringLength** attribute.

Q9. ★Which feature of ASP.NET 4.0 allows web server administrators to monitor the performance of websites?
A9. In order to increase the number of Web sites that can be hosted on a single server, many hosters run multiple ASP.NET applications in a single worker process. However, if multiple applications use a single shared worker process, it is difficult for server administrators to identify an individual application that is experiencing problems.

ASP.NET 4 leverages new resource-monitoring functionality introduced by the CLR. To enable this functionality, you can add the following XML configuration snippet to the **aspnet.config** configuration file.

```
<?xml version="1.0" encoding="UTF-8" ?>
  <configuration> <runtime> <appDomainResourceMonitoring enabled="true"/>
</runtime>
 </configuration>
```

Note: The **aspnet.config** file is in the .NET Framework folder

As a result, with ASP.NET 4, administrators now have a higher level of view over the resource consumption of individual applications running in a single worker process.

Q10. ★Can Meta Tags be set through the Page directive?
A10. ASP.NET 4.0 allows setting some meta tags through the Page directive.

See the example below:

```
<%@ Page Language="C#" AutoEventWireup="true" CodeFile="Default.aspx.cs"
Inherits="_Default" Keywords="Crackerjack, Interview, Questions, Answers,.NET"
Description="Here goes the description" %>
```

The attributes Keywords and Description allow doing this.

When the page renders, the source code of the web page appears like this:

```
<head id="Head1" runat="server">
<title>Untitled Page</title>
<meta name="keywords" content=" Crackerjack, Interview, Questions, Answers,.NET " />
<meta name="description" content=" Here goes the description" />
</head>
```

Q11. ★★What is URL Routing in ASP.NET 4.0?
A11. ASP.NET 4 adds built-in support for using routing with Web Forms. Routing lets you configure an application to accept request URLs that do not map to physical files. Instead, you can use routing to define URLs that are meaningful to users and that can help with search-engine optimization (SEO) for your application. For example, the URL for a page that displays product categories in an existing application might look like the following example:

http://www.dotnetuncle.com/products.aspx?categoryid=12

By using routing, you can configure the application to accept the following URL to render the same information:

http://www.dotnetuncle.com/products/software. See here that this URL makes more meaning to search engines.

Q12. ★★Which feature of ASP.NET 4.0 allows better control over the IDs of controls?

A12. Before the advent of ASP.NET 4.0, IDs of controls used to look hefty after rendering, somewhat like this:

ctl00_ContentPlaceHolder1_ParentPanel_NamingPanel1_TextBox1

The new **ClientIDMode** property lets you specify more precisely how the client ID is generated for controls. You can set the *ClientIDMode* property for any control, including for the page. Possible settings are the following:

AutoID – This is equivalent to the algorithm for generating **ClientID** property values that was used in earlier versions of ASP.NET.
Static – This specifies that the *ClientID* value will be the same as the ID without concatenating the IDs of parent naming containers. This can be useful in Web user controls. Because a Web user control can be located on different pages and in different container controls, it can be difficult to write client script for controls that use the *AutoID* algorithm because you cannot predict what the ID values will be.
Predictable – This option is primarily for use in data controls that use repeating templates. It concatenates the ID properties of the control's naming containers, but generated *ClientID* values do not contain strings like "ctlxxx". This setting works in conjunction with the **ClientIDRowSuffix** property of the control. You set the **ClientIDRowSuffix** property to the name of a data field, and the value of that field is used as the suffix for the generated *ClientID* value. Typically you would use the primary key of a data record as the *ClientIDRowSuffix* value.
Inherit – This setting is the default behavior for controls; it specifies that a control's ID generation is the same as its parent.

Q13. ★What are the features of the ASP.NET 4.0 Chart control?

A13. The ASP.NET 4.0 Chart control includes the following features:

1. 35 distinct chart types.
2. An unlimited number of chart areas, titles, legends, and annotations.
3. A wide variety of appearance settings for all chart elements.
4. 3-D support for most chart types.
5. Smart data labels that can automatically fit around data points.
6. Strip lines, scale breaks, and logarithmic scaling.
7. More than 50 financial and statistical formulas for data analysis and transformation.
8. Simple binding and manipulation of chart data.
9. Support for common data formats such as dates, times, and currency.
10. Support for interactivity and event-driven customization, including client click events using Ajax.
11. State management.
12. Binary streaming.

Q14. ★★How does ASP.NET 4.0 prevent XSS attacks?

A14. XSS attacks can be prevented in ASP.NET 4.0 based applications using HTML encoded code expressions.

The native

```
<%= expression %>
```

Can now be written as...

```
<%: expression %>
```

CHAPTER 8 – ASP.NET Security

Q1. ★How does the NoBot control help prevent invalid spams on websites?

A1. Automated bots conquer websites with spam, submitting comment forms without any user interaction. The NoBot control in the ASP.NET AJAX Control Toolkit can help fight those bots. The NoBot stops the postback of the current ASP.NET web form if at least one of these conditions is met:

- ✓ Client browser fails to solve a JavaScript puzzle (for instance when JavaScript is deactivated)
- ✓ The user submitted the form very quick
- ✓ The IP address of the client submitted the form too often in a particular time period

Q2. ★What is a Captcha control?

A2. A Captcha control dynamically creates textual or numeric images on the screen, which need to be read by human beings and consequently entered into an input box, before a form can be submitted. These images are generated in such a way that they generally can't be read by optical reading algorithms. The intent is to stop automatic spams and bots to submit unwanted inputs into web pages.

There are several free and paid Captcha controls available. There is one available in the ASP.NET Ajax Control Toolkit too.

Q3. ★★★How to use Code Access Security (CAS) for ASP.NET?

A3. ASP.NET website administrators may use the CAS trust levels with ASP.NET in order to separate applications from each other that are running on a common web server. Further, it can be used to specify which resource type can be allowed to a particular web application and which privileged operations can be performed by an application. This requirement is very important in environments where multiple web applications reside on a shared web server.

Basically there are three things to do:

1. Understand and evaluate the requirements
2. Identify a Trust Level
3. Set the application to use the right Trust Level

Trust Level may be High, Medium, Low or Minimal. The Trust Level can be set as follows, in the web.config file:

```
<system.web>
...
  <trust level="Medium" originUrl="" />
...
</system.web>
```

Q4. ★★★Which Trust Level is required by ASP.NET to access SQL databases?

A4. ASP.NET 2.0 applications (and above) set with Medium Trust Level can access SQL Server databases. Running at Medium trust is mainly helpful for setups where more than one applications run on a common server and you need to make sure that applications are separated from each other and also separated from common system modules.

Limitations of Medium Trust Level: If you run applications in Medium trust, there is no access to unmanaged code, and file access is restricted to the application's own virtual directory hierarchy. Further, applications do not have access to the system registry, the event log, and the OLE DB data sources. In such cases, the code is unable to use reflection, and it can only communicate with specific servers identified by the **originUrl** attribute on the **<trust>** element.

In order to configure applications so that they run with Medium trust, you need to set the **level** attribute of the **<trust>** element in the machine-level Web.config as shown below.

```
<location allowOverride="false">
 <system.web>
 ...
   <trust level="Medium" originUrl="" />
 ...
 </system.web>
</location>
```

After setting the **allowOverride="false"** on the **<location>** element, this prevents an individual application's Web.config file from overriding the machine-wide policy. Use the **originUrl** attribute to determine which HTTP server's applications it may communicate with.

Q5. ★★★Is there a way to create and set customized Trust Levels in CAS for ASP.NET?

A5. Yes this is quite possible. In order to use a custom trust level, a custom trust files needs to be created. This file has to be based on the existing trust file that most closely matches the application's requirements.

Further, to create a custom level and configure an application, the following steps have to be carried out:

1. Figure out the trust level that satisfies most of your application's permission requirements. This level will eventually lay out the ground rules, which may further be customized.
2. Next, copy the trust policy file for that level to create a custom trust policy file, for example, the file web_CustomTrust.config may be copied.
3. Add the additional permissions required to this file. For example, to add the registry permission to a custom trust policy file, you may do the following:

   Add a <SecurityClass> element.

   ```
    <SecurityClass Name="RegistryPermission"
    Description="System.Security.Permissions.RegistryPermission, mscorlib,
Version=2.0.0.0,
    Culture=neutral, PublicKeyToken=b77a5c561934e089"/>
   ```

   Add an <IPermission> element to the "ASP.Net" named permission set.

   ```
    <PermissionSet class="NamedPermissionSet"
   ```

```
         version="1"  Name="ASP.Net">
                    ...
           <IPermission
           class="RegistryPermission"  version="1"  Unrestricted="true" />
           </PermissionSet>
```

4. Further, configure the application's root Web.config file in order to make the application use the custom trust policy file. This may be done as follows:

```
<location allowOverride="false">
 <system.web>
  <securityPolicy>
   <trustLevel name="Custom"
           policyFile="web_CustomTrust.config" />
  </securityPolicy>
  <trust level="Custom" originUrl="" />
 </system.web>
</location>
```

Q6. ★★★Should you keep sensitive data in configuration files? How to encrypt sensitive data in config files?

A6. Developers and Architects normally keep passwords and other sensitive data such as IP address, usernames, and connection strings etc. in the web.config or machine.config files. However, such an approach makes the sensitive data vulnerable to security threats such as hacker attacks or an insider's malicious intents.

So what is the best way and place to keep this data? Well, sensitive data may be kept in the config files, provided it is encrypted.

In ASP.NET 2.0 *(and above)*, the **Aspnet_regiis**.exe tool may be used with the -pe *(provider encryption)* option to encrypt sections of the Machine.config and Web.config files.

In order to encrypt the connectionStrings section by using the DPAPI provider with the machine key store (the default configuration), the following set of commands have to be run on the .NET command prompt.

aspnet_regiis -pe "connectionStrings" -app "/MachineDPAPI"

-prov "DataProtectionConfigurationProvider"

The points below will help you understand how the command works:

✓ The –pe attribute instructs the configuration section to encrypt
✓ The -app attribute specifies the Web application's virtual path. If the application is nested, you need to specify the nested path from the root directory, for example "/test/aspnet/MachineDPAPI"
✓ The -prov attribute specifies the provider name

Further, note that the .NET Framework 2.0 (and above) supports

RSAProtectedConfigurationProvider and **DPAPIProtectedConfigurationProvider** protected configuration providers, which you use with the Aspnet_regiis.exe tool. So this means there are basically two providers to achieve the goal of encrypting.

RSAProtectedConfigurationProvider - This is the default provider. It uses the RSA public key encryption to encrypt and decrypt data. Use this provider to encrypt configuration files for use on multiple Web servers in a Web farm.

DPAPIProtectedConfigurationProvider - This provider uses the Windows Data Protection API (DPAPI) to encrypt and decrypt data. Use this provider to encrypt configuration files for use on a single Windows Server.

The following sections of a config file usually contain sensitive information that should be encrypted:

- ✓ <appSettings> - Custom application settings.
- ✓ <connectionStrings> - Connection strings.
- ✓ <identity> - Web application identity. Can contain impersonation credentials.
- ✓ <sessionState> - Contains connection string for out of process session provider.

You do not need any special steps for decryption, because the ASP.NET runtime takes care of this for you. Further, note that you cannot use the Aspnet_regiis.exe tool and protected configuration to encrypt the following sections in Web.config and Machine.config:

<processModel>, <runtime>, <mscorlib>, <startup>, <system.runtime.remoting>, <configProtectedData>, <satelliteassemblies>, <cryptographySettings>, <cryptoNameMapping>, and <cryptoClasses>.

> **Tip**: If some data needs to be encrypted for these sections, use the **Aspnet_setreg.exe** tool.

As a default, the **DataProtectionConfigurationProvider** is configured to use DPAPI with the machine store. To use it with the user store, include a **<configProtectedData>** section in your Web.config file and specify the **useMachineProtection** attribute as **false**. Further, a unique provider name has to be specified. This is shown below:

```
<configProtectedData>
 <providers>
  <add useMachineProtection="false" keyEntropy=""
  name="MyUserDataProtectionConfigurationProvider"
  type="System.Configuration.DpapiProtectedConfigurationProvider, System.Configuration,
  Version=2.0.0.0, Culture=neutral, PublicKeyToken=b03f5f7f11d50a3a" />
 </providers>
```

```
</configProtectedData>
```

Next, run the following command from a .NET command prompt to encrypt the
<connectionStrings> section:

```
aspnet_regiis–pe "connectionStrings"–app "/UserDPAPI" -prov
"MyUserDataProtectionConfigurationProvider
```

Q7. ★★How to create a service account for ASP.NET?
A7. In order to create a service account for ASP.NET applications, perform the
following steps:

1. Create a Windows account
2. Run the following **Aspnet_regiis.exe** command to assign the relevant
    ASP.NET permissions to the account:

    ```
    aspnet_regiis.exe -ga MachineName\UserName
    ```

    In Windows 2003 Server, running the Aspnet_regiis.exe -ga command
    adds the account to the IIS_WPG group. The IIS_WPG group provides
    the Log on as batch job permission and further makes sure that the
    required file system permissions are given.

3. Make use of the Local Security Policy tool to grant the Windows account
    the Deny logon locally user right. This reduces the privileges of the
    account and prevents anyone logging onto Windows locally with the
    account.
4. Use IIS Manager to create an application pool running under the new
    account's identity and assign the ASP.NET application to the pool.

Q8. ★★★Is it possible to lock all the web.config files located on a web server?
A8. Yes this is possible by making the right set of changes in the machine.config
file. In order to lock the configuration settings for all the Web applications on a
Web server to prevent an individual application from overriding them, you need to
put the configuration settings inside a <system.web> element nested within a
<location> element in the machine-level Web.config file, and then set the
allowOverride attribute to false.

The following example enforces the use of Windows authentication for all Web
applications on the server.

```
<location allowOverride="false">
  <system.web>
   <authentication mode="Windows"/>
  </system.web>
</location>
```

In case the locking is to be done for a specific Web application, use the path
attribute on the <location> element to identify the Web application.

In case it is important that there are no cross-application breaches, it is advised to configure the Web.config file in the /VDirName directory for locking the configuration rather than using the path attribute to lock the specific Web application.

```
<location path="Default Web Site/VDirName">
  <system.web>
   <authentication mode="Windows"/>
   <identity impersonate="false"/>
  </system.web>
</location>
```

In case the path is specified, it must be completely qualified and should include the Web site name and virtual directory name.

Q9. ★★Can you use Windows authentication to connect to an SQL Server?
A9. In order to use Windows authentication, configure the SQL Server correctly and then use a connection string that has either "Trusted_Connection=Yes", or "Integrated Security=SSPI". This is shown in the following code. The two strings are same and both result in Windows authentication.
"server=MySQL; Integrated Security=SSPI; database=Northwind"
"server=MySQL; Trusted_Connection=Yes; database=Northwind"

Q10. ★★What is CSRF?
A17. CSRF stands for Cross Site Request Forgery. It's also called as XSRF. It is also known as **one-click attack** and **session riding**. It involves malicious attacks to a website whereby unauthorized commands are carried from a user that a website trusts. Note that XSS attacks *(which are Cross Site Scripting Attacks)* exploit the trusted external websites, whereas CSRF exploits the trust a user has in a browser.

CHAPTER 9 – ADO.NET

Q1. ★What is ADO.NET?
A1. ADO.NET is a part of the Microsoft .NET Framework. This framework provides the set of classes that deal with data communication between various layers of the software architecture and the database. It provides a continuous access to different data source types such as SQL Server versions 7, 2000, 2005, 2008 and SQL Azure. It also provides connectivity options to data sources through OLE DB and XML. Connectivity may be established with other databases like Oracle, MySQL etc. as well.

ADO.NET has the ability to separate data access mechanisms, data manipulation mechanisms and data connectivity mechanisms.

ADO.NET introduces along with it the disconnected architecture. In a disconnected architecture, data may be stored in a DataSet. It contains providers for connecting to databases, commands for execution and retrieval of results.

The classes for ADO.NET are stored in the DLL System.Data.dll.

Q2. ★★★Can the performance of a web application be improved through connection pooling?
A2. The connection pooling process allows a live connection between the web server and the database (wherever this database is located) so that multiple users don't have to create a connection to the backend individually. This essentially means that a connection pool allows sharing of the connection. Otherwise, opening a database connection for each user takes a heavy toll on both the web server and the database server. Each connection takes some amount of memory. So if multiple users have to connect to the database, multiple connections will drastically slow down the performance of the server.

Connection pooling allows a set of database connections open. These connections can be shared amongst multiple users. When a connection is requested, this connection object is temporarily removed from the pool. Once the connection is closed, it is returned back to the pool.

As such, connection pooling is enabled by default for **OleDb** and **SqlClient** connections.

In order to ensure connection pooling takes place, the connection string for each connection to the database should be the same. The common connection string may be placed in the web.config file. Further, to ensure that the performance is good, it is always recommended to close the connection as soon as it has been consumed, so that the connection is put back to the connection pool.

Q3. ★★ What are the connection pool options available to a SQL connection string?
A3. The following are the connection pool options available to a SQL connection string:

Connection Lifetime – This option destroys a connection after some seconds. The default value for this is 0, and this signifies that connections should never be destroyed.

Connection Reset – This option indicates whether a connection has to be reset whenever they are returned to a pool.

Enlist – This option indicates whether a connection has to be automatically enlisted in the current transaction context. This is set to true by default.

Max Pool Size – This signifies the maximum number of connections allowed in a single connection pool. This is set to 0 by default.

Pooling – This option tells whether connection pooling is enabled or disabled. By default, its value is set to true.

Q4. ★What is a connection object in ADO.NET? How to connect to a database in .NET?
A4. A Connection object in ADO.NET is used to establish a connection between a program *(the program may be a windows page, a web page, a windows service, a web service etc.)* and the database. The connection is open just long enough to get or update data. By quickly opening, then closing a connection, the server resources are used as little as possible. See code below on how to open a connection between UI and database.

Example (VB.NET):

```
Dim objectConn as SqlClient.SqlConnection
Dim strConn as String
Try
'First, create a connection object
objectConn=New SqlClient.SqlConnection()

'Next, build the Connection String
strConn &="Data Source=(local
strConn &="Initial Catalog=DatabaseName;"
strConn &= "User ID=admin;"
strConn &= "Password=;"

'Note here that the connection string may also be passed as a parameter
'to the connection string object during instantiation

objectConn.ConnectionString = strConn
objectConn.Open() 'Open the Connection

'The connection is now open
'Write your vb.net code here for operations on the database
objectConn.Close()

Catch Ex As Exception
MessageBox.Show(Ex.Message)
End Try
```

Q5. ★What are Connection Strings?

A5. A connection string has a group of semi-colon-separated attributes. Every .Net Data Provider connection string looks different; depending on the type of .NET Data Provider you need to use and which attributes are set for each different type of database system. An example, the connection string below is an example of what you use to connect to a local SQL Server. See that every parameter is separated by a semicolon.

Data Source=(local);Initial Catalog=Northwind;User ID=sa;Password=;

The connection string shown below is an example of how to connect to a Microsoft Access 2000 database using the OleDbConnection object in System.Data.OleDb.

Provider=Microsoft.Jet.OleDb.4.0;Data Source=C:\Northwind.mdb

Parameters in a Connection String - The parameters depend on the data provider is being used.

Server - The name of the SQL Server to which connection has to be established through ADO.NET. This is the name of the system that is running SQL server. We may use "local" or "localhost" for local computer. In case we are using named instances of SQL server, then the parameter would contain the computer name, followed by a backslash, followed by a named instance of the SQL server.

Database - The name of the database to which connection is to be established.

User ID - A user ID configured in the SQL Server by the SQL Server administrator.

Password - As the attribute name suggests, this is the password associated with the user id.

> **Note**: Connection string may also contain the Windows NT account security settings. This is done by passing the parameter "integrated security=true".

Q6. ★What is a command object in ADO.NET? How to use a command object in .NET?

A6. **ADO.NET Command Object** - The Command object is similar to the old ADO command object. It is used to store SQL statements that need to be executed against a data source. The Command object can execute a SELECT statements, INSERT, UPDATE, or DELETE statements, stored procedures, or any other statement understood by the database.

Example (VB.NET):

```
'Code below in VB.NET ...
Dim ObjCom as SqlClient.SqlCommand
ObjCom.SqlConnection(strCon)
ObjCom.Connection.Open()
```

```
ObjCom.CommandText = "Select * from tblSample"
ObjCom.ExecuteNonQuery()
```

SqlCommand objects are not used much when we use datasets and data adapters. Following are some properties of the SqlCommand class...

Connection Property - This property contains data about the connection string. It must be set on the SqlCommand object before it is executed. For the command to execute properly, the connection must be open at the time of execution.

CommandText Property - This property specifies the SQL string or the Stored Procedure.

```
objCom.CommandText = "Insert into t_Bar (Whisky_Id, Whisky_Name values ('W00555','Highland
Park')"
```

Parameters Collection - If we want to update values in the Employees table above, but we do not know the values at design time, we make use of placeholders. These are variables prefixed with "@" symbol. Our code will look like this...

```
objCom.CommandText = "Insert into t_Bar (Whisky_Id, Whisky_Name) values (@Whisky_Id,
@Whisky_Name)
```

Next, we have to create parameters that will be used to insert values into the placeholders. For this, we need to add parameters to the parameters collection of the SqlCommand object. This is done so that the values added through the parameters collection & placeholders get included in the SQL statement. Here, parameters mean the parameters to be passed to the SQL statement/Stored Procedures, not the method's parameters.

In order to add parameters to the SqlCommand object, we write the following code...

```
objCom.CommandText = "Insert into t_Bar (Whisky_Id, Whisky_Name) values (@Whisky_Id,
@Whisky_Name)"

objCom.Parameters.Add("@Whisky_Id", txtwhiskyid.text)

objCom.Parameters.Add("@Whisky_Name", txtwhiskyname.text)
```

ExecuteNonQuery Method - Once the connection is open, we run the query in the SqlCommand object using the ExecuteNonQuery method.

Example (VB.NET):

```
objConnection.Open()
objCom.ExecuteNonQuery()
objConnection.Close()
```

Q7. ★ What is SelectCommand in ADO.NET?

A7. **Select Command Property** - This property is used to hold the SQL command that is used to retrieve data from the data source. The CommandText and Connection are properties of the Select Command property. CommandType is also a property of Select Command.

Example (VB.NET):

```
Dim da as new SqlDataAdapter
da.SelectCommand = New SqlCommand( )
With da.SelectCommand
. Connection = objConnection
. CommandText = "select * from employees"
End With
```

Q8. ★What is a SqlCommandBuilder in ADO.NET?

A8. **SqlCommandBuilder** class in ADO.NET provides the feature of reflecting the changes made to a DataSet or an instance of the SQL Server data. When an instance of the SqlCommandBuilder class is created, it automatically generates Transact-SQL Statements for the single table updates that occur. The object of the SqlCommandBuilder acts as a listener for RowUpdating events, whenever the **DataAdapter** property is set.

The SqlCommandBuilder object automatically generates the values contained within the SqlDataAdapter's InsertCommand, UpdateCommand and DeleteCommand properties based on the initial SelectCommand. The advantage here is that you will not need to write SqlCommand & SqlParameter Types explicitly.

Basically the command builder object builds these objects on the fly. The command builder object actually reads the metadata of the method called. After the builder object reads the underlying schema of the adapter's method, it autogenerates an underlying insert, update & delete command object.

Example (C#):

```
DataSet ds = new DataSet();
SqlConnection cn = new SqlConnection("strSomeConnectionString");
// Autogenerate Insert, Update & Delete commands
SqlDataAdapter da = new SqlDataAdapter("Select from t_Something", cn);
SqlCommandBuilder scb = new SqlCommand(da);

//Fill the dataset
da.Fill(ds,"t_Something");
```

Q9. ★What is a DataView in ADO.NET?

A9. **DataView** - Just like we have Views in SQL *(in our backend)*, we have DataView object in ADO.NET. A dataview object represents bindable, customized view of a DataTable object. Operations like Sorting, Filtering, Searching, Editing and Navigation may be performed on a DataView object. In scenarios like retrieval of a subset of data from a DataTable, we may make use of DataViews to get this data. Note that the **DefaultView** property of a DataTable returns the Default data view for the DataTable. In case a custom view of a

DataTable has to be created on a DataView, then the **RowFilter** property of the DataView is set to the DefaultView.

A dataview may also be used to sort data that resides in it in ascending or descending order. Below is code on how to sort data in a dataview in ascending or descending order...

Example (C#):

```
DataView objdv = new DataView();
objdv.Sort("ColumnName Asc|Desc");
```

Q10. ★★What is DataRelation object in ADO.NET? How to use a DataRelation between two columns in ADO.NET?
A10. In order to set the relationship between two or more than two columns, ADO.NET provides the **DataRelation** class. When a DataRelation object is created, it assists to enforce some constraints on the relationships between columns. The constraint may be a **Unique constraint** that ensures that a column will have no duplicate value in the table. A **Foreign Key** constraint may be used to enforce **Referential Integrity**. The Unique property may be set by setting the Unique property of a DataColumn to True. This may also be done by adding an instance of the UniqueConstraint class to the DataRelation object. As a part of the foreign key constraint, we may specify referential integrity rules that are applied at three places

✓ When a parent record is updated
✓ When a parent record is deleted
✓ When a change is rejected or accepted.

A DataRelation object permits to establish a parent-child relationship between two or more tables inside a DataSet object. The easiest way to create a DataRelation between two tables in a DataSet is to setup a primary key - foreign key relationship between the columns of a table.

See the example, where a DataRelation has been setup between the Employee table and the Salary table.

Example (VB.NET):

```
Dim Conn As SqlConnection
Dim da As SqlDataAdapter
Dim ds As DataSet
Dim RowParent As DataRow
Dim RowChild As DataRow

Conn = New _
SqlConnection(ConfigurationSettings.Appsettings("SomeConnectionStringWrittenInWeb.Config"))
da = New SqlDataAdapter("SELECT * FROM Employees", Conn)
ds = New DataSet()

Try
```

```
  Conn.Open()
  da.Fill( ds,"Employees")
  da.SelectCommand = New SqlCommand("SELECT * FROM Salary", Conn)
  da.Fill(ds, "Salary")
Catch ex As SqlException
  Response.Write(ex.ToString())
Finally
  Conn.Dispose()
End Try

'Next, Let us create a Data Relationship
ds.Relations.Add("Employee_Salary", ds.Tables("Employees").Columns("EmployeeID"), _
ds.Tables("Salary").Columns("EmployeeID"))
'Display the Employee and Child Salary in the Form
'Say we have a Label in the form
For each RowParent in ds.Tables("Employees").Rows

  lblRelation.Text &= RowParent("Emp_Name")
  For each RowChild in RowParent.GetChildRows("Employee_Salary")
   lblRelation.Text &= "<br/>" & RowChild("Sal_Amount")
  Next
Next
```

Q11. ★What is Diffgram in ADO.NET? When do we use Diffgram?

A11. A **DiffGram** is an XML format. It is used to identify current and original versions of data elements. A **DataSet** may use a DiffGram format to load and persist the contents, and further to serialize its contents for porting across a network connection. Whenever a DataSet is written as a DiffGram, the DataSet populates the DiffGram with all the important information to accurately recreate the contents. Note that schema of the DataSet is not recreated. This includes column values from the Current and the Original row versions, row error information, and row order.

Q12. ★★What is a Typed Dataset in ADO.NET? Why do we use a Typed DataSet? What is the difference between a Typed and an UnTyped DataSet?

A12. **Typed DataSet** - When a created DataSet derives from the DataSet class, that applies the information contained in the XSD to create a Typed class, this DataSet is said to be a Typed Dataset. Information from the schema which comprises the tables, columns, and rows is created and compiled to a new DataSet derived from the XSD. The Typed DataSet class features all functionality of the DataSet class. This may be used with methods that take an instance of the DataSet class as a parameter.

Note that an **UnTyped DataSet** does not have any schema. It is exposed simply as a mere collection.

How to create a Typed DataSet? –

Write click your project in the Solution Explorer.

Click Add New Item.

Select DataSet.

This adds a new XSD to the project. The schema created may be viewed as an XML. When this xsd file is compiled, two files are created by Visual Studio. The first file that contains the .vb or .cs extension contains the information about the proxy class. This class contains methods & properties that are required to access the database data. The second file has an extension **xsx** and this contains information about the layout of the XSD.

Q13. ★How to run a stored procedure from .NET code?
A13. Use the **Command** object and its **ExecuteNonQuery** method to run a DDL or DCL statement of SQL. First, create a connection object and a command object, and configure these objects for the statement you wish to execute. Open the database connection. Call ExecuteNonQuery on the command. Close the connection.

Example (T-SQL):

Suppose we have to insert FirstName into a table t_Employees. Our Store procedure is:

```
Create Procedure dbo.InsertFirstName
(
@FirstName varchar(30)
)
as
Insert Into t_Employees values (@FirstName)
```

VB.NET code below, to pass FirstName to this Stored Procedure

```
Dim cmRunProc as New SqlCommand("dbo.InsertFirstName", objCon)
cmRunProc.CommandType = CommandType.StoredProcedure
cmRunProc.Parameters.Add("@FirstName", txtFirstName.Text)
objCon.Open()
cmdRunProc.ExecuteNonQuery()
objCon.Close()
```

Q14. ★Which connection provider is generally preferred to connect to Oracle databases?
A14.The **OracleConnection** object comes with the Microsoft.NET Framework. Oracle database connections use the OracleDataAdapter object to perform commands and return data. This connection object was introduced in Microsoft .NET Framework version 1.1. This is a Microsoft product.

Additionally, Oracle provides the **ODP.NET Provider** (Oracle Data Provider) which can be used for connecting to different versions of Oracle such as 9i, 10g, 11g. This is an Oracle product.

Q15. ★How to read the records of a table in a database, using a datareader?
A15.In order to read data from the database, you first make a connection object (SqlConnection, etc) and then open it.

```
string connString = "server=ALCOHOL; database=RUM;uid=drunkdj; pwd=";
SqlConnection conn = new SqlConnection(connString);
conn.Open();
```

Next, you go ahead and create a command using this connection and the command text.

```
string cmdString = "select * from cocktails";
SqlCommand cmd = new SqlCommand(cmdString, conn);
```

After this, you execute the command using the ExecuteReader() method. The ExecuteReader method returns the object of type IDataReader.

```
SqlDataReader reader = cmd.ExecuteReader();
```

In order to read the individual records using the data reader, the records have to be traversed one by one. For this, you can invoke the **Read()** method which returns Boolean to indicate if there exists a next record. If this returns true, then the DataReader reads the next row. After this, the fields of this the fields may be accessed by specifying the column names (or indexes) in its indexers.

```
while(reader.Read())
{
txtData.Text += reader["currencyId"].ToString();
txtData.Text += ", ";
txtData.Text += reader["name"].ToString();
txtData.Text += "
";
}
```

Once this is run, the database connection has to be closed.

```
conn.Close();
```

Q16. ★**What is the difference between a DataReader and a DataAdapter?**
A16. The difference is as follows:

A **DataReader** is meant for read-only purpose in a forward-only direction. It exhibits a faster performance than a **DataAdapter**.

If a DataReader is used, a connection has to be opened and closed explicitly, where as if DataAdapter is used; the connection is automatically opened and closed.

Q17. ★**What does the ExecuteNonQuery() method return?**
A17. The ExecuteNonQuery() method returns the number of rows (an integer value) affected by the SQL statement that has been run. This method can be used to carry out catalog operations (for example, querying the structure of a database or creating database objects such as tables), or to change the data in a database without using a DataSet by executing UPDATE, INSERT, or DELETE statements.

Q18. ★**What is the difference between Execute Reader, Execute Scalar and ExecuteNonQuery methods?**
A18. The following points elaborate the differences:

ExecuteReader() - The ExecuteReader() method is used to return the set of rows after the execution of an SQL Query or a stored procedure, by using command object.

ExecuteScalar() – The ExecuteScalar() method is used to return the single record, on the execution of the SQL Query or stored procedure, by using command object.

ExecuteNonQuery() – In case the command or stored procedure performs a DML command such as INSERT, DELETE or UPDATE, then the ExecuteNonQuery() method is used. This method returns an integer specifying the number of rows inserted, deleted or updated.

Q19. ★What is a SQL Injection?
A19. A SQL Injection is a malicious way of attacking SQL databases.
Input web forms may appear to be simple to use, and attackers might misuse certain input fields and try to gain unauthorized access to databases. For example, a web form may ask users to enter the user name and password for logging in. The following may be the corresponding SQL Statement:

Select from users where username='someuser' and password='somepassword'

This seems to be safe but it isn't.

The attacker might enter the username as follows

'OR 1 > 0 –

When the above value is entered, the resulting SQL statement is as follows

Select from users where username='' OR 1 > 0and password=''

This comments out the password portion of the statement, and returns all the user names in the users table. This kind of injection opens the gates for unauthorized users to gain access to your database.

To avoid a SQL injection, the SQL string should be parsed and the - - should be removed.

Semicolons can also be used for SQL Injections. For example, the input below can get into your database:

'OR 1>0; Delete Users; --

Q20. ★What are the different types of data sources an application can connect to?
A20. An application may connect to several types of data sources such as SQL Databases *(Microsoft SQL Server, MySQL, Oracle Database Server, Sybase, MS Access etc.)*, a flat file *(such as a .txt file, a .csv file etc.)*, Excel files etc.

Q21. ★★What is the SqlPipe class?

A21. A **SqlPipe** class allows managed stored procedures running in-process on a SQL Server database to return results back to the caller. This class cannot be inherited. An instance of this class may be made available to managed stored procedures through the Pipe property of the SqlContext class.

Q22. ★★What is a CLR Stored Procedure?

A22. A **CLR Stored Procedure** is a procedure that runs as a managed object in the SQL Server's memory. These CLR Stored Procedures give all the benefits of a managed object. CLR stored procedures addresses issues such as memory leaks, bugs etc. As these are managed objects, they run as per the specifications of the CLR. CLR Stored procedures can replace standard stored procedures. A key advantage of using CLR Stored is that it can easily benefit from a huge number of .NET classes available. The CLR Stored Procedures while executing complex logic, intense string operations or string manipulations, cryptography, fetching system resources, file management, etc. Further, CLR Stored Procedures make sure that there is type safety and good memory management. **Below are the steps to create a simple CLR Stored Procedure:**

1. Open Visual Studio (Version 2008)

2. Click new project

3. Select Database Projects

4. Select SQL Server Project

5. Here, you may select an existing database or a new database reference.

6. When OK is clicked, you will be asked to enable SQL/CLR debugging on the connection that has been selected. After this step, the project will appear in the Solution Explorer of Visual Studio.

7. Right Click on the Project, Click on Add, Select Stored Procedure

8. Add a new procedure from the templates. Give an appropriate name to this template. Say you named the file as 'test', you will see a file by the name test.cs.

9. Set "context connection=true" in the connection string when create a new SQL connection. Note that this CLR Stored Procedure will be a part of the database, so there won't be any need to specify a connection string.

10. Click on Build Menu >> Click on Build Solution.

11. Click on Build Menu >> Deploy Solution. This will ensure the CLR Stored Procedure is deployed in the SQL Server.

12. In your SQL Server Management Studio, Select the database >> Programmability.

13. Right click on Stored Procedures. Click on Refresh.

14. Right click on Assemblies. Click on Refresh.

15. Run the following on your SQL Window:

    a.   sp_configure 'clr enabled', 1

    b.   Reconfigure

Q23. ★★When to use CLR Stored Procedures and when to use Standard Stored Procedures?
A23. The developers may decide when to use what. The following points may be taken into consideration whilst making a decision in favor of CLR Stored Procedures.

1. In case the program requires extensive business rules and highly complex business logic, use CLR Stored Procedures.
2. When there will be a huge toll on the CPU usage, use CLR Stored Procedures because they are precompiled.
3. Say there are tasks such as cryptography, access to system resources, such tasks might be difficult to achieve using standard stored procedures.
4. You may convert your Extended Stored Procedures to CLR Stored Procedures, because CLR Stored Procedures are better in terms of performance.
5. In case a high level of data safety is required, CLR Stored Procedures are nearly impossible to crack.

Q24. ★What is a Data Provider?
A24. A **Data Provider** is essential a group of functions in DLLs that can be used to establish a connection with a database. For example, an Oracle Data Provider can be used to connect to Oracle databases, an OLE DB Provider can be used to connect to MS Excel, or MS Access.

CHAPTER 10 – AJAX

Q1. ★What is AJAX?
A1. **Ajax** stands for Asynchronous Javascript & XML. It is a web technology through which a postback from a client *(browser)* to the server goes partially, which means that instead of a complete postback, a partial postback is triggered by the Javascript XmlHttpRequest object. In such a scenario, web-application users won't be able to view the complete postback progress bar shown by the browser. In an AJAX environment, it is Javascript that starts the communication with the web server.

Ajax technology in a website may be implemented by using plain Javascript and XML. Code in such a scenario may tend to look little complex, for which the AJAX Framework in .NET can be embedded in ASP.NET web applications.

In addition to XML & Javascript, AJAX is also based on DOM - the Document Object Model technology of browsers through which objects of the browser can be accessed through the memory heap using their address.

JSON - Javascript Object Notation is also one of the formats used in AJAX, besides XML.

So basically, in an AJAX-based web application, the complete page does not need to reload, and only the objects in context of ajaxification are reloaded.

Ajax technology avoids the browser flickering.

Q2. ★Can Ajax be implemented in browsers that do not support the XmlHttpRequest object?
A2. Yes. This is possible using remote scripts.

Q3. ★Can AJAX technology work on web servers other than IIS?
A3. Yes, AJAX is a technology independent of web server the web application is hosted on. Ajax is a client *(browser)* technology.

Q4. ★Which browsers support the XmlHttpRequest object?
A4. Internet Explorer 5.0+, Safari 1.2, Mozilla 1.0/Firefox, Opera 8.0 +, Netscape 7, Chrome 1.0.

Q5. ★★How to we create an XmlHttpRequest object for Internet Explorer? How is this different for other browsers?
A5. For Internet Explorer, an ActiveXObject is used for declaring an XmlHttpRequest object in Javascript.

```
//Code as below for IE:
xmlHttpObject = new ActiveXObject("Msxml2.XMLHTTP");
//For Other browsers, code as below:
xmlHttpObject = new XmlHttpRequest();
```

> **Note**: XmlHttpObject used above is simply a variable that holds the XmlHttpRequest object for the respective browsers.

Q6. ★★★What are the properties of the XmlHttpRequest object? What are the different types of readyStates in Ajax?

A6. Read on:

i) **onreadyStateChange** - This function is used to process the reply from the web server.

ii) **readyState** - This property holds the response status of the web server. There are 5 states:

- ✓ 0 - request not yet initialized

  1 - request now set

  2 - request sent

  3 - request processing

  4 - request completes

iii) **responseText** - Has the data sent back by the web server

Code snippet below shows an example how these properties are used to implement Ajax :

```
xmlHttpObject.onreadystatechange=function()
{
if(xmlHttpObject.readyState==4)
{
document.Form1.time.value=xmlHttpObject.responseText;
}
}
```

Q7. ★What is the ASP.NET Ajax Framework? What versions have been released so far?

A7. ASP.NET AJAX is a free framework to implement Ajax in asp.net web applications, for quickly creating efficient and interactive Web applications that work across all popular browsers.

The Ajax Framework is powered with

1 - Reusable Ajax Controls

2 - Support for all modern browsers

3 - Access remote services and data from the browser without tons of complicated script.

Versions of Ajax released

1 - ASP.NET Ajax Framework 1.0 *(earlier release to this was called the Atlas)*
2 - ASP.NET Ajax Framework 1.0 was available as a separate download for ASP.NET 2.0
3 – Ajax Framework for .NET comes as an integral part in .NET 3.5 *(and above)*
4 – Microsoft has also launched Ajax Library 4.0

Q8. ★ What are Ajax Extensions?

A8. The ASP.NET Ajax Extensions are set of Ajax-based controls that work in ASP.NET 2 *(or above)* based applications.

They also need the Ajax runtime which is actually the Ajax Framework 1.0.

ASP.NET Ajax Extensions 1.0 have to be downloaded to run with ASP.NET 2.0.

The new ASP.NET 3.5 Framework comes with the Ajax Library 3.5 (containing the Ajax Extensions 3.5). So in order to use the latest Ajax, simply download .NET 3.5 Framework.

Summary:

- ✓ ASP.NET Ajax Extensions 1.0 -> For ASP.NET 2.0
- ✓ ASP.NET Ajax Extensions 3.5 -> For ASP.NET 3.5

Note that the latest Ajax Framework comes as a part of ASP.NET 4.0.

Q9. ★ What is the ASP.NET Control Toolkit?

A9. Besides the Ajax Framework (which is the Ajax engine) and Ajax Extensions (which contain the default Ajax controls), there is a toolkit called the Ajax Control Toolkit available for use & download (for free). This is a collection of rich featured, highly interactive controls, created as a joint venture between Microsoft & the Developer Community. It is an open-source software.

Q10. ★ What is Dojo?

A10. Dojo is a third-party javascript toolkit for creating rich featured applications. Dojo is an Open Source DHTML toolkit written in JavaScript. It builds on several contributed code bases (nWidgets, Burstlib, f(m)), which is why we refer to it sometimes as a "unified" toolkit. Dojo aims to solve some long-standing historical problems with DHTML which prevented mass adoption of dynamic web application development.

Q11. ★ ★ How to handle multiple or concurrent requests in Ajax?

A11. For concurrent requests, declare separate XmlHttpRequest objects for each request. For example, for request to get data from an SQL table1, use something like this...

xmlHttpObject1.Onreadystatechange = functionfromTable1();

And to get data from another table (say table2) at the same time, use

xmlHttpObject2.Onreadystatechange = functionfromTable2();

Ofcourse, the XmlHttpObject needs to be opened & parameters passed too, like as shown below:

xmlHTTPObject1.open("GET","http://"localhost// " + "Website1/Default1.aspx" true);

Note that the last parameter "true" used above means that processing shall carry on without waiting for any response from the web server. If it is false, the function shall wait for a response.

Q12. ★**How to create an AJAX website using Visual Studio?**
A12. Using Visual Studio Web Developer Express 2005 & versions above it, Ajax based applications may easily be created. Note that the Ajax Framework & Ajax Extensions should be installed (In case of VS 2005). If using Visual Studio 2008 Web Developer Express or above, Ajax comes along with it (so no need of a separate installation).

Steps: Start Visual Studio, Click on File → New Website -> Under Visual Studio Installed templates → Select ASP.NET Ajax-Enabled Site. Enter a location & select OK.

Q13. ★**What is the role of ScriptManager in Ajax?**
A13. The **ScriptManager** class is the heart of ASP.NET Ajax. Before elaborating more on ScriptManager, note that ScriptManager is class and a control *(both)* in Ajax.

The ScriptManager class in ASP.NET manages Ajax Script Libraries, partial page rendering functionality and client proxy class generation for web applications and services. By saying client proxy class, this means an instance of the Ajax runtime is created on the browser.

This class is defined in the System.Web.Extensions.dll. You will find this DLL in your system's Global Assembly Cache at C:\Windows\Assembly (For XP)

The ScriptManager control *(that we may drag on a web form)* is actually an instance of the ScriptManager class that we put on a web page. The ScriptManager manages all the ASP.NET Ajax controls on a web page. Following tasks are taken care by the ScriptManager class:

1 - Managing all resources (all objects/controls) on a web page

2 - Managing partial page updates

3 - Download Ajax Script Library to the client (means to the browser). This needs to happen so that Ajax engine is accessible to the browsers javascript code.

4 - Interacting with UpdatePanel Control, UpdateProgress Control.

5 - Register script (using RegisterClientScriptBlock)

6 - Information whether Release OR Debug script is sent to the browser

7 - Providing access to Web service methods from the script by registering Web services with the ScriptManager control

8 - Providing access to ASP.NET authentication, role, and profile application services from client script after registering these services with the ScriptManager control

9 - Enable culture specific display of clientside script.

10 - Register server controls that implement IExtenderControl and IScriptControl interfaces.

> **Important**: The ScriptManager class' **EnablePartialRendering** property is true by default.

Q14. ★★Can we override the EnablePartialRendering property of the ScriptManager class?
A14. Yes. But this has to be done before the init event of the page (or during runtime after the page has already loaded). Otherwise an **InvalidOperationException** will be thrown.

Q15. ★★How to use multiple ScriptManager controls in a web page?
A15. No. It is not possible to use multiple ScriptManager control in a web page. In fact, any such requirement never comes in because a single ScriptManager control is enough to handle the objects of a web page.

Q16. ★★What is the difference between RegisterClientScriptBlock, RegisterClientScriptInclude and RegisterClientScriptResource?
A16. For all three, a script element is rendered after the opening form tag. Following are the differences:
1 - RegisterClientScriptBlock - The script is specified as a string parameter.
2 - RegisterClientScriptInclude - The script content is specified by setting the src attribute to a URL which points to a script file.
3 - RegisterClientScriptResource - The script content is specified with a resource name in an assembly. The src attribute is automatically populated with a URL by a call to an HTTP handler that retrieves the named script from the assembly.

Q17. ★★★What are type/key pairs in client script registration? Can there be 2 scripts with the same type/key pair name?
A17. When a script is registered by the **ScriptManager** class, a type/key pair is created to uniquely identify the script.

For identification purposes, the type/key pair name is always unique for identifying a script. Hence, there may be no duplication in type/key pair names.

Q18. ★What is an UpdatePanel Control?
A18. An UpdatePanel control is a holder for server side controls that need to be partial postbacked in Ajax cycle. All controls residing inside the UpdatePanel will be partial postbacked. Below is a small example of using an UpdatePanel.

```
<script runat="server">
protected void btn1_Click(object sender, EventArgs e)
{
  lb123.Text = "new";
}
</script>
```

```
<asp:ScriptManager ID="ScriptManager1" runat="server">
 </asp:ScriptManager>
<asp:UpdatePanel ID="UpdatePanel1" runat="server">
 <ContentTemplate>
 <asp:Button id="btn1" runat="server" text="click"/>
<br/>
 <asp:Label id="lb123" runat="server" text="Old"/>
</ContentTemplate>
</UpdatePanel>
```

As you see here after running the snippet above, there won't be a full postback exhibited by the web page. Upon clicking the button, the postback shall be partial. This means that contents outside the UpdatePanel won't be posted back to the web server. Only the contents within the UpdatePanel are refreshed.

Q19. ★★What are the modes of updating in an UpdatePanel? What are Triggers of an UpdatePanel?

A19. An UpdatePanel has a property called **UpdateMode**. There are two possible values for this property: 1) Always 2) Conditional

If the UpdateMode property is set to **Always**, the UpdatePanel control's content is updated on each postback that starts from anywhere on the webpage. This also includes asynchronous postbacks from controls that are inside other UpdatePanel controls, and postbacks from controls which are not inside UpdatePanel controls.

If the UpdateMode property is set to **Conditional**, the UpdatePanel control's content is updated when one of the following is true:

1 - When the postback is caused by a trigger for that UpdatePanel control.

2 - When you explicitly call the UpdatePanel control's Update() method.

3 - When the UpdatePanel control is nested inside another UpdatePanel control and the parent panel is updated.

When the **ChildrenAsTriggers** property is set to true and any child control of the UpdatePanel control causes a postback. Child controls of nested UpdatePanel controls do not cause an update to the outer UpdatePanel control unless they are explicitly defined as triggers for the parent panel.

Controls defined inside a **<Triggers>** node have the capability to update the contents of an UpdatePanel.

If the ChildrenAsTriggers property is set to false and the UpdateMode property is set to Always, an exception is thrown. The ChildrenAsTriggers property is intended to be used only when the UpdateMode property is set to Conditional.

Q20. ★★How to control how long an Ajax request may last?

A20. Use the ScriptManager's **AsyncPostBackTimeout** Property.

For example, if you want to debug a web page but you get an error that the page request has timed out, you may set <asp:ScriptManager id="ScriptManager1" runat="server" AsyncPostBackTimeout="9000"/>

where the value specified is in seconds.

Q21. ★What are the limitations of Ajax?
A21. 1) An Ajax Web Application tends to confuse end users if the network bandwidth is slow, because there is no full postback running. However, this confusion may be eliminated by using an UpdateProgress control in tandem.
2) Distributed applications running Ajax will need a central mechanism for communicating with each other

Q22. ★★How to make sure that the contents of an UpdatePanel update only when a partial postback takes place (and not on a full postback)?
A22. Make use of **ScriptManager.IsInAsyncPostBack** property *(returns a boolean value)*

Q23. ★How to trigger a postback on an UpdatePanel from Javascript?
A23. Call the __**doPostBack** function. ASP.NET runtime always creates a javascript function named __doPostBack(eventTarget, eventArgument) when the web page is rendered. A control ID may be passed here to specifically invoke updating of the UpdatePanel.

Q24. ★Which request is better with AJAX, Get or Post?
A24. AJAX requests should use an HTTP GET request while retrieving data where the data does not change for a given URL requested. An HTTP POST should be used when state is updated on the server. This is in line with HTTP idempotency recommendations and is highly recommended for a consistent web application architecture.

Q25. ★What is the Microsoft Ajax Content Delivery Network (CDN)?
A25. The Microsoft Ajax **Content Delivery Network** *(CDN)* hosts many famous third party JavaScript libraries such as **JQuery** that allow developers to seamlessly add them to the Web applications. For example, you can start using JQuery which is hosted on the CDN website simply by adding a <script> tag to your page that points to ajax.aspnetcdn.com.

By taking advantage of the CDN, you can significantly improve the performance of your Ajax applications. The contents of the CDN are cached on servers located around the world. In addition, the CDN enables browsers to reuse cached third party JavaScript files for web sites that are located in different domains.

The CDN supports SSL *(HTTPS)* in case you need to serve a web page using the Secure Sockets Layer.

The CDN hosts the following third party script libraries which have been uploaded, and are licensed to you, by the owners of those libraries. These are:

✓ JQuery (www.jquery.com)

- ✓ JQuery UI (www.jqueryui.com)
- ✓ JQuery Mobile (www.jquerymobile.com)
- ✓ JQuery Validation (www.jquery.com)
- ✓ JQuery Cycle (www.malsup.com/jquery/cycle/)
- ✓ Ajax Control Toolkit (owned by the Outercurve Foundation – www.outercurve.org)

The Microsoft Ajax CDN also includes the following libraries which have been uploaded by Microsoft:

1. ASP.NET Ajax
2. ASP.NET MVC JavaScript Files

CHAPTER 11 – Comparison Interview Questions

Q1. ★What's the difference between Classic ASP and ASP.NET?
A1. **Major difference:** Classic ASP is interpreted whereas ASP.NET is compiled. In case the code is changed, ASP.NET recompiles.

Other differences: ASP works with VB as the language. ASP.NET works with VB.NET & C# as the languages *(Also supported by other languages that run on the .NET Framework).*

ASP.NET is the web technology that comes with the Microsoft .NET Framework. The main process in ASP.NET is called **aspnet_wp.exe** that accesses system resources. ASP.NET was launched in 2002 with version 1.0. Subsequent versions are 1.1, 2.0, 3.5, 4.0. The ASP.NET 4.5 version is to be released soon. ASP.NET is built using thousands of objects, ordered in the System namespace. When an ASP.NET class is compiled, it's called an assembly.

In Classic ASP, complex functionalities are achieved using COM components that are nothing but component objects created using VB 6, C++ etc, and are usually in a DLL format. These components provide an exposed interface to methods in them, to the objects that reference these components. Last version of classic ASP is version 3.0. The Classic ASP has 7 main objects - **Application, ASPError, ObjectContext, Request, Response, Server, and Session**.

Q2. ★What is the difference between ADO and ADO.NET?
A2. The old **ADO** *(ActiveX Data Object)* has evolved to ADO.NET in the .NET Framework. The ADO.NET object is a lightweight object. The ADO **Recordset** was a huge object in ADO. It provided the ability to support multiple types of cursors. It provided fast lightweight **"firehose"** cursor and also supported a disconnected client-side cursor that supported tracking, optimistic locking, and automatic batch updates of a central database. However, all of this functionality was difficult to customize.
ADO.NET breaks the functionality of the ADO object to multiple classes, thereby allowing a focused approach to developing code. The ADO.NET **DataReader** is equivalent to the "firehose" cursor. The DataSet is a disconnected cache with tracking and control binding functionality. The **DataAdapter** provides the ability to completely customize how the central data store is updated with the changes to a DataSet.

Q3. ★What's the difference between Structure, Class and Enumeration?
A3. **Structures** and **Enumerations** are Value-Types. This means, the data that they contain is stored as a stack on the memory. **Classes** are Reference-Types, means they are stored as a heap on the memory.

Structures are implicitly derived from a class called **System.ValueType**. The purpose of System.ValueType is to override the virtual methods defined by System.Object. So when the runtime encounters a type derived from System.ValueType, then stack allocation is achieved. When we allocate a structure type, we may also use the **new** keyword. We may even make a constructor of a structure, but, remember, **A No-argument constructor for a structure is not possible**. The structure's constructor should always have a parameter.

So if we define the following structure

```
struct MyStruct
{
  public int y,z;
}
```
and we create a structure type
```
MyStruct st = new MyStruct();
```

In case of a class, no-argument constructors are possible. Class is defined using the **class** keyword.

> **Note**: A struct cannot have an instance field, whereas a class can.

```
class A
{
  int x = 5; //No error ...
}
```

```
struct
{
  int x = 5; //Syntax Error
}
```

A class can inherit from one class. **Multiple inheritance not possible**. A Structure cannot inherit from another structure.

Enum is the keyword used to define an enumeration. An enumeration is a distinct type consisting of a set of named constants called the enumerator list. Every enumeration has an underlying type. The default type is "int". **Note: char can't be the underlying data type for enum**. First value in enum has value 0; each consequent item is increased by 1.

```
enum colors {red, green, blue, yellow};
```

Here, red is 0, green is 1, blue is 2 and so on.
An explicit casting is required to convert an enum value to its underlying type

```
int x = (int)colors.yellow;
```

Q4. ★★What is the difference between an abstract class and an interface?
A4. If a class is to serve the purpose of providing common fields and members to all subclasses, we create an **Abstract class**. For creating an abstract class, we make use of the **abstract** keyword. Such a class cannot be instantiated. Syntax below:

```
abstract public class Vehicle { }
```

Above, an abstract class named Vehicle has been defined. We may use the fields, properties and member functions defined within this abstract class to create child classes like Car, Truck, and Bike etc. that inherit the features defined within the abstract class. To prevent directly creating an instance of the class

Vehicle, we make use of the abstract keyword. To use the definitions defined in the abstract class, the child class inherits from the abstract class, and then instances of the Child class may be easily created. Further, we may define abstract methods within an abstract class (analogous to C++ pure virtual functions) when we wish to define a method that does not have any default implementation. It's then in the hands of the descendant class to provide the details of the method. There may be any number of abstract methods in an abstract class. We define an abstract method using the **abstract** keyword. If we do not use the abstract keyword, and use the **virtual** keyword instead, we may provide an implementation of the method that can be used by the child class, but this is not an abstract method.

Remember, abstract class can have an abstract method, that does not have any implementation, for which we use the abstract keyword, OR the abstract class may have a virtual method, that can have an implementation, and can be overriden in the child class as well, using the **override** keyword. Read example below.

Example: Abstract Class with Abstract method
```
namespace Automobiles
{
 public abstract class Vehicle
 {
  public abstract void Speed() //No Implementation here, only definition
 }
}
```

Example: Abstract Class with Virtual method
```
namespace Automobiles
{
 public abstract class Vehicle
 {
  public virtual void Speed() //Can have an implementation, that may be overriden in child class
  {
   ...
  }
 }
}

Public class Car : Vehicle
{
Public override void Speed()
//Here, we override whatever implementation is there in the abstract class
 {
   ... //Child class implementation of the method Speed()
 }
}
}
```

An **Interface** is a collection of semantically related abstract members. An interface expresses through the members it defines, the behaviors that a class needs to support. An interface is defined using the keyword **interface**. The members defined in an interface contain only definition, no implementation. The members of an interface are all public by default; any other access specifier cannot be used. See code below:

Public interface IVehicle //As a convention, an interface is prefixed by letter I
{
  Boolean HasFourWheels()
}

Now, it is time to discuss the difference between Abstract Class and Interface?

1) A class may inherit only one abstract class, but may implement multiple numbers of Interfaces. Say a class named Car needs to inherit some basic features of a vehicle; it may inherit from an Abstract class named Vehicle. A car may be of any kind, it may be a vintage car, a sedan, a coupe, or a racing car. For these kinds of requirements, say a car needs to have only two seats (means it is a coupe), then the class Car needs to implement a member field from an interface, that we make, say ICoupe.

2) Members of an abstract class may have any access modifier, but members of an interface are public by default, and can't have any other access modifier.

3) Abstract class methods may OR may not have an implementation, while methods in an Interface only have a definition, no implementation.

Q5. ★Explain the access specifiers Public, Private, Protected, Friend, Internal, Default
A5. The main purpose of using access specifiers is to provide security to the applications. The availability *(scope)* of the member objects of a class may be controlled using access specifiers.

1. PUBLIC

As the name specifies, it can be accessed from anywhere. If a member of a class is defined as public then it can be accessed anywhere in the class as well as outside the class. This means that objects can access and modify public fields, properties, methods.

2. PRIVATE

As the name suggests, it can't be accessed outside the class. It's the private property of the class and can be accessed only by the members of the class.

3. FRIEND/INTERNAL

Friend & Internal mean the same. Friend is used in VB.NET. Internal is used in C#. Friends can be accessed by all classes within an assembly but not from outside the assembly.

4. PROTECTED

Protected variables can be used within the class as well as the classes that inherit this class.

5. PROTECTED FRIEND/PROTECTED INTERNAL

The Protected Friend can be accessed by Members of the Assembly or the inheriting class, and ofcourse, within the class itself.

6. DEFAULT

A Default property is a single property of a class that can be set as the default. This allows developers that use your class to work more easily with your default property because they do not need to make a direct reference to the property. Default properties cannot be initialized as Shared/Static or Private and all must be accepted at least on argument or parameter. Default properties do not promote good code readability, so use this option sparingly.

Q6. ★What is the difference between Overriding and Shadowing?
A6. Both Overriding and Shadowing are ways to alter the behavior of members of a base class. Shadowing is a VB.NET concept. In C#, this concept is called **Hiding**, though there is a difference between the two.

When we do **shadowing**, we provide a new implementation to the base class member without overriding it. We may shadow a base class member in a derived class, by using the keyword **shadows**. The access level, return type, and the signature (means the datatypes of the arguments passed & the order of the types) of the derived class members which are shadowed, may differ from the base class.

In C#, we may achieve shadowing using the keyword **new**. However, in shadowing, the access level, the signature, return type of the derived class must be **same** as the base class.

Overriding is the concept of providing a new implementation of derived class member as compared to its based class. In VB.NET, we do overriding using the **overrides** keyword, while in C#, overriding is achieved using the **override** keyword. For a class member to be overridable, we use the keyword **virtual** while defining it (in C#), and we use the keyword **overridable** (in VB.NET), though if we leave out specifying the overridable keyword, the member is overridable by default.

Q7. ★What's the difference between a class and an object?
A7. In any object oriented language, an object is the backbone of everything that we see. A class is a blueprint that describes how an instance of it *(object)* will behave. To create a class, we define it in a "Code File", with an extension *.cs or *.vb. We make use of the keyword **class**.

Example (C#):

```
Lets create a class named Laptop
public class Laptop
{
  private string sbrand;
  public Laptop() {}
  public Laptop(string name)
```

```
  {
    sbrand = name;
  }
}
```

From our code that references this class, we write...
Laptop lp = new Laptop("Vaio"); //Passing a variable to the class constructor

Once the class object is created, the object may be used to invoke the member functions defined within the class. We may allocate any number of objects using the **new** keyword. The new keyword returns a reference to an object on the heap. This reference is not to the actual object itself. The variable being referred is stored on a stack for usage in the application. When we allocate an object to a heap, it's managed by the .NET runtime. The garbage collector takes care of the object by removing it from the heap, when it is no longer reachable by any part of the code.

Q8. ★★What is the difference between Shared and Static?
A8. They both mean the same. Shared is used in VB.NET. Static is used in C#.

When the **static** keyword is used to declare a class, the member in context must be directly invoked from the class, rather than from the instance. Consider the following example.

//Consider writing the following line of code...
Console obj = new Console();
obj.Writeline("Vishal likes static members"); //This line doesn't print

//This doesn't work, because WriteLine is a static method defined in the class Console
//The Console class is a static class

To use static members, give a reference to the exact class, as an instance in this case won't work.

To make this work, write:
Console.Writeline("Vishal likes static members");

To work with members of static classes, no need to create their instances.

Static Member - A class member declared with the keyword **static** is a static member. A static member is owned by the class, not by its instances (objects of the class).

Note that static members are actually class members, while non-static members are instance members (means they are owned by the instances). Both in C# & VB.NET, we may create static/shared events, properties, fields and functions.

> **Note:** Indexers in C# cannot be declared static. Also note that Static member functions cannot access non-static members directly.

Q9. ★What is the difference between value type and reference type? Can a value type contain NULL values?

A9. In simple words, all value based types are allocated on the **stack**, while all reference based types are allocated on the **heap**. What does this mean? A value type contains the actual value. A reference type contains a reference to the value. When a value type is assigned to another value type, it is copied. When a reference type is assigned to another reference type, a reference is assigned to the value.

By saying stack, we mean things are kept one on top of the other. We keep track of each value at the top. By saying heap, we mean things are kept in a mashed order. We keep track of each value by its address that is referenced by a pointer to it.

All value types are implicitly derived from System.ValueType. This class actually overrides the implementation in System.Object, the base class for all objects which is a reference type itself.

Data types such as integers, floating point numbers, character data, Boolean values, Enumerations and Structures are examples of Value Types. Classes, Strings, Arrays are examples of Reference Types.

A value type may not contain NULL values. Reference types may contain NULL values.

It is not possible to derive new types from Value Types. This is possible in Reference types. However, Value Types like Structures can implement interfaces.

Q10. ★What is the difference between MSIL and CIL?
A10. **MSIL** is the name given to the intermediate language in .NET Framework Beta, 1.0 and 1.1. From version 2.0 onwards, the intermediate language is called **CIL**. We can say, MSIL is the old name. MSIL stands for Microsoft Intermediate Language. CIL stands for Common Intermediate Language. It's actually a low level human readable language implementation of CLI.

There is not much difference between the two. Compilers like vbc.exe and csc.exe compile the code into intermediate language. CIL is the name submitted by Microsoft to the European Computer Manufacturer's Association(ECMA) as a standard.

Q11. ★What is the difference between a DLL and an EXE?
A11. In .NET, an assembly may become a DLL or an EXE. Yet, there is a major underlying difference between the two.

An **EXE** is an executable file that may run on its own. It is independent. Where as a **DLL** is a Dynamic Link Library, that binds to an exe, or another DLL at runtime.

A DLL has an exposed interface, through which members of the assembly may be accessed by those objects that require it.

A DLL runs in tandem with the application space in memory, as the application references it. An EXE is independent, and runs as an independent process.

Q12. ★What is the difference between a Class Library and a Namespace?

A12. **Class Library** is another major entity of the .NET Framework *(the other being the CLR)*. This library gives the program access to runtime environment. The class library consists of lots of prewritten code that all the applications created in .NET will use. The code for all the elements like forms, controls actually comes from the class library. The main class library in .NET is **mscorlib.dll**. This library contains a large number of core types that encapsulate a wide variety of common tasks. When a .NET application, there is automatic access to this library. We may view the class libraries provided by the .NET Framework by seeing the Global Assembly Cache *(Go to C:\Windows\Assembly OR C:\Winnt\Assembly)*.

Namespace is a grouping of related types contained in an assembly. For example, the System.Drawing namespace consists of classes, methods that are grouped together to achieve similar tasks.

Note that a single assembly like mscorlib.dll may contain any number of namespaces. In fact, namespaces may be nested (means a namespace within a namespace) to arrange classes in a hierarchical fashion.

Also note that any language that works on the .NET environment, targets the same set of namespaces & types provided by the .NET framework.

Q13. ★What is the difference between String and StringBuilder?
A13. Both **String** and **StringBuilder** are classes used to handle strings.

The most common operation with a string is concatenation. This activity has to be performed very efficiently. When we use the "String" object to concatenate two strings, the first string is combined to the other string by creating a new copy in the memory as a string object, and then the old string is deleted. This process is a little long. Hence we say **"Strings are immutable"**.

When we make use of the "StringBuilder" object, the **Append** method is used. This means, an insertion is done on the existing string. Operation on StringBuilder object is faster than string operations, as the copy is done to the same location. Usage of StringBuilder is more efficient in case large amounts of string manipulations have to be performed.

Q14. ★★What is the difference between Web Services and Remoting?
A14. Both **Remoting** and **Web Services** are ways of communication between applications.

Remoting - In remoting, the applications involved in the communication process may be located on the same computer, different computers in a same or different network. In remoting, both applications know about each other. A proxy of an application object is created on the other application.

Web Services - Communication between applications using web services is platform independent and programming independent. The application that consumes the web service, simply accesses it, without needing to know how this web service has actually been implemented & created.

Here are some of the major differences:

- ✓ ASP.NET Web Services may be accessed using HTTP only. Remoting objects may be accessed over any protocol like TCP, SMTP, HTTP
- ✓ Web Service are Stateless, whereas Remoting has support for both stateless and with-state environment, which is achieved using **Singleton** and **Singlecall activation** respectively.

- ✓ ASP.NET provides good support to create Web Services. They are easy to deploy. In comparison, Remoting is little complex.
- ✓ Web services may be considered very reliable, due to the fact that they are hosted on IIS. In remoting, if IIS isn't used, then methods like plumbing have to be used to ensure the application reliability.
- ✓ In .NET, when we create an application that consumes a web service, the web service may or may not be built using .NET. But while implementing Remoting in .NET, both the applications must be built in .NET.
- ✓ Using web services, only a limited number of types may be serialized (XML). Using Remoting, objects like SOAP objects, Binary objects & XML Objects may be serialized.

Q15. ★What is the difference between a Public Assembly and a Private Assembly?
A15. An assembly is the basic building block in .NET. It is the compiled format of a class that contains Metadata, Manifest & Intermediate Language code.

An assembly may be either **Public** or **Private**. A public assembly means the same as **Shared Assembly**.

Private Assembly - This type of assembly is used by a single application. It is stored in the application's directory or the applications sub-directory. There is no version constraint in a private assembly.

Shared Assembly or Public Assembly - A shared assembly has version constraint. It is stored in the Global Assembly Cache (GAC). GAC is a repository of shared assemblies maintained by the .NET runtime. It is located at **C:\Windows\Assembly OR C:\Winnt\Assembly**. The shared assemblies may be used by many applications. To make an assembly a shared assembly, it has to be **strongly named**. In order to share an assembly with many applications, it must have a strong name.

A **Strong Name** assembly is an assembly that has its own identity, through its version and uniqueness.

In order to convert a private assembly into a shared assembly (a strongly named assembly), carry out the steps below.

1) Create a strong key using the **sn.exe** tool. This is used to create a cryptographic key pair. The key pair that is generated by the Strong Name tool can be kept in a file or we can store it in your local machine's **Crytographic Service Provider** *(CSP)*. For this, go to the .NET command interpreter, and type the following...

sn -k C:\samplekey.snk

This will create a strong key and save it to the location C:\samplekey.snk

2) If the key is stored in a file, just like we have done above, we use the attribute **AssemblyKeyFileAttribute**. This belongs to the namespace **System.Reflection.AssemblyKeyFileAttribute**. If the key was in the CSP, we would make use of System.Reflection.AssemblyKeyNameAttribute.

Go to the assemblyinfo.vb file of your project. Open this file. Make the following changes in this file...

<assembly: assemblykeyfileattribute("C:\samplekey.snk")>

We may write this in our code as well, like this...

```
Imports System.Reflection
<assembly: assemblykeyfileattribute("C:\samplekey.snk")>
Namespace StrongName
 Public class Sample
 End Class
End Namespace
```

3) Build your project. Your assembly is now strongly named.
Installing the Shared assembly in GAC...
Go to .NET command interpreter, use the tool gacutil.exe
Type the following...

gacutil /i sampleclass.dll

To uninstall it, use **gacutil /u** sampleclass.dll. Visual Studio.NET provides a GUI tool for viewing all shared assemblies in the GAC.

Q16. ★★What is the difference between Trace and Debug?
A16. **Trace and Debug** - There are two main classes that deal with tracing - Debug and Trace. They both work in a similar way - the difference is that tracing from the Debug class only works in builds that have the DEBUG symbol defined, whereas tracing from the Trace class only works in builds that have the TRACE symbol defined. Typically this means that you should use System.Diagnostics.Trace.WriteLine for tracing that you want to work in debug and release builds, and System.Diagnostics.Debug.WriteLine for tracing that you want to work only in debug builds.

Tracing is actually the process of collecting information about the program's execution. Debugging is the process of finding & fixing errors in our program. Tracing is the ability of an application to generate information about its own execution. The idea is that subsequent analysis of this information may help us understand why a part of the application is not behaving as it should and allow identification of the source of the error.

We shall look at two different ways of implementing tracing in .NET via the **System.Web.TraceContext** class via the **System.Diagnostics.Trace** and

System.Diagnostics.Debug classes. Tracing can be thought of as a better alternative to the response.writes we used to put in our classic ASP3.0 code to help debug pages.

If we set the Tracing attribute of the Page Directive to True, then Tracing is enabled. The output is appended in the web form output. Messages can be displayed in the Trace output using **Trace.Warn & Trace.Write**.

NOTE The only difference between Trace.Warn & Trace.Write is that the former has output in red color. If the trace is false, there is another way to enable tracing. This is done through the application level. We can use the web.config file and set the trace attribute to true. Here we can set <trace enabled=false .../>

Note that the Page Directive Trace attribute has precedence over the application level trace attribute of **web.config**. While using application level tracing, we can view the trace output in the **trace.axd** file of the project.

Q17. ★What is the difference between Server.Transfer and Response.Redirect?

A17. Both "Server" and "Response" are objects of ASP.NET. **Server.Transfer** and **Response.Redirect** both are used to transfer a user from one page to another. But there is an underlying difference.

//Usage of Server.Transfer & Response.Redirect
```
Server.Transfer("Page2.aspx");
Response.Redirect("Page2.aspx");
```

The **Response.Redirect** statement sends a command back to the browser to request the next page from the server. This extra round-trip is often inefficient and unnecessary, but this established standard works very well. By the time Page2 is requested, Page1 has been flushed from the server's memory and no information can be retrieved about it unless the developer explicitly saved the information using some technique like session, cookie, application, cache etc.

The more efficient **Server.Transfer** method simply renders the next page to the browser **without an extra round trip**. Variables can stay in scope and Page2 can read properties directly from Page1 because it's still in memory. This technique would be ideal if it wasn't for the fact that the browser is never notified that the page has changed. Therefore, the address bar in the browser will still show "Page1.aspx" even though the Server.Transfer statement actually caused Page2.aspx to be rendered instead. This may occasionally be a good thing from a security perspective; it often causes problems related to the browser being out of touch with the server. Say, the user reloads the page, the browser will request Page1.aspx instead of the true page (Page2.aspx) that they were viewing. In most cases, Response.Redirect and Server.Transfer can be used interchangeably. But in some cases, efficiency or usability may be the deciding factor in choosing.

Q18. ★What is the difference between Server.Transfer and Server.Execute?

A18. Both **Server.Transfer and Server.Execute** were introduced in Classic ASP 3.0 (and still work in ASP.NET).

When **Server.Execute** is used, a URL is passed to it as a parameter, and the control moves to this new page. Execution of code happens on the new page. Once code execution gets over, the control returns to the initial page, just after where it was called. However, in the case of **Server.Transfer,** it works very much the same, the difference being the execution stops at the new page itself (means the control isn't returned to the calling page).

In both the cases, the URL in the browser remains the first page URL (doesn't refresh to the new page URL) as the browser isn't requested to do so.

Q19. ★What is the difference between Authorization and Authentication?
A19. Both **Authentication and Authorization** are concepts of providing permission to users to maintain different levels of security, as per the application requirement.

Authentication is the mechanism whereby systems may securely identify their users. Authentication systems depend on some unique bit of information known only to the individual being authenticated and the authentication system.

Authorization is the mechanism by which a system determines what level of access a particular authenticated user should have to secure resources controlled by the system.

When a user logs on to an application/system, the user is first Authenticated, and then Authorized.

ASP.NET has 3 ways to Authenticate a user:

1) **Forms Authentication**

2) **Windows Authentication**

3) **Passport Authentication** (This is obsolete in .NET 2.0)

The 4th way is "None" (means no authentication)

The Authentication Provider performs the task of verifying the credentials of the user and decides whether a user is authenticated or not. The authentication may be set using the web.config file.

Windows Authentication provider is the default authentication provider for ASP.NET applications. When a user using this authentication logs in to an application, the credentials are matched with the Windows domain through IIS.

There are 4 types of Windows Authentication methods:

1) **Anonymous Authentication** - IIS allows any user
2) **Basic Authentication** - A windows username and password has to be sent across the network (in plain text format, hence not very secure).
3) **Digest Authentication** - Same as Basic Authentication, but the credentials are encrypted. Works only on IE 5 or above

4) **Integrated Windows Authentication** - Relies on Kerberos technology, with strong credential encryption
5) **Forms Authentication** - This authentication relies on code written by a developer, where credentials are matched against a database. Credentials are entered on web forms, and are matched with the database table that contains the user information.

Authorization in .NET - There are two types:

FileAuthorization - this depends on the NTFS system for granting permission

UrlAuthorization - Authorization rules may be explicitly specified in web.config for different web URLs.

Q20. ★What is the difference between ExecuteScalar and ExecuteNonQuery? What is ExecuteReader?

A20. **ExecuteScalar** - Returns only one value after execution of the query. It returns the first field in the first row. This is very light-weight and is perfect when all your query asks for is one item. This would be excellent for receiving a count of records (Select Count(*)) in an SQL statement, or for any query where only one specific field in one column is required.

ExecuteNonQuery - This method returns no data at all. It is used majorly with Inserts and Updates of tables. It is used for execution of DML commands.

Example (C#):

```
SqlCommand cmd = new SqlCommand("Insert Into t_SomeTable Values('1','2')",con);
//note that con is the connection object
con.Open();
cmd.ExecuteNonQuery(); //The SQL Insert Statement gets executed
```

ExecuteReader - This method returns a DataReader which is filled with the data that is retrieved using the command object. This is known as a forward-only retrieval of records. It uses our SQL statement to read through the table from the first to the last record.

Q21. ★What is the difference between a DataReader and Dataset in ADO.NET?

A21. A DataReader works in a connected environment, whereas DataSet works in a disconnected environment.

A **DataReader** object represents a forward only, read only access to data from a source. It implements IDataReader & IDataRecord interfaces. For example, The SQLDataReader class can read rows from tables in a SQL Server data source. It is returned by the **ExecuteReader** method of the SQLCommand class, typically as a result of a SQL Select statement. The DataReader class' **HasRows** property can be called to determine whether the DataReader retrieved any rows from the source. This can be used before using the **Read** method to check whether any data has been retrieved.

Example (VB.NET):

```
Dim objCmd as New SqlCommand("Select * from t_Employees", objCon)
objCon.Open()
Dim objReader as SqlDataReader
objReader = objCom.ExecuteReader(CommandBehavior.CloseConnection)
If objReader.HasRows = True then
 Do While objReader.Read()
   ListBox1.Items.Add(objReader.GetString(0) & vbTab & objReader.GetInt16(1))
 Loop
End If
objReader.Close()
```

Note: **XmlReader** object is used for Forward only Read only access of

A **DataSet** represents an in-memory cache of data consisting of any number of inter-related DataTable objects. A DataTable object represents a tabular block of in-memory data. Further, a DataRow represents a single row of a DataTable object. A Dataset is like a mini-database engine, but its data is stored in the memory. To query the data in a DataSet, we can use a DataView object.

Example (VB.NET):

```
Dim objCon as SqlConnection = New
SqlConnection("server=(local);database=NameOfYourDb;user id=sa; password=;)
Dim da as New SqlDataAdapter
Dim ds as DataSet = New DataSet
da.SelectCommand.Connection = objCon 'The Data Adapter manages on its own, opening &
closing of connection object
da.SelectCommand.CommandText = "Select * from t_SomeTable"
da.Fill(ds,"YourTableName")
```

Suppose you want to bind the data in this dataset to a GridView

```
Gridview1.DataSource = ds
Gridview1.DataMember = "YourTableName"
Gridview1.Databind()
```

A22. The **Clone()** method returns a **new array** *(a shallow copy)* object containing all the elements in the original array. The **CopyTo()** method copies the elements into another **existing array**. Both perform a shallow copy.

Q23. ★What is the difference between a Thread and Process?
A23. A **process** is a collection of virtual memory space, code, data, and system resources. A **thread** is code that is to be serially executed within a process. A processor executes threads, not processes, so each application has at least one process, and a process always has at least one thread of execution, known as the primary thread. A process can have multiple threads in addition to the primary thread. Prior to the introduction of multiple threads of execution, applications were all designed to run on a single thread of execution.

When a thread begins to execute, it continues until it is killed or until it is interrupted by a thread with higher priority (by a user action or the kernel's thread scheduler). Each thread can run separate sections of code, or multiple threads can execute the same section of code. Threads executing the same block of code maintain separate stacks. Each thread in a process shares that process's global variables and resources.

Q24. ★What is the difference between Delete and Truncate?
A24. The DELETE table command in SQL logs the deletes thus making the delete operations slow. On the other hand, the TRUNCATE table does not log any information but it logs information about the deallocation of the data page of the table. This makes the TRUNCATE table command perform faster.

Secondly, the DELETE table can be rolled back while TRUNCATE cannot be rolled back.

Thirdly, the DELETE table command can have criteria whereas the TRUNCATE table command cannot.

Further, note that the TRUNCATE table cannot have triggers whereas the Delete table command can.

CHAPTER 12 – Silverlight

Q1. ★Does Silverlight work in Desktop applications, or only in Web Applications?
A1. Silverlight works on Web, Desktop and Mobile platforms.

Q2. ★Which languages can be used to create Silverlight based applications?
A2. XAML (It is a declarative language to create shapes, controls, texts), C#, VB.NET. XAML is somewhat similar to HTML but more powerful. Further, XAML is XML based, and hence has to follow XML rules.

Q3. ★How to create a button in XAML?
A3. Read on:

```
<Grid x:Name="LayoutRoot" Background="White">
<Button Width="60" Height="30">Click Here</Button>
</Grid>
```

> **Note**: Visual Studio can be directly used to create the button, instead of typing the code above.

Q4. ★What is Silverlight?
A4. Silverlight is a software framework by Microsoft, meant to develop applications to browsers, desktops and mobile through a text-based markup language called XAML. Though it is similar to Adobe Flash, a key difference between Flash and XAML is that Flash is a compiled application where as XAML is text based. Because of its textual nature, search engines can easily identify such applications and index the content.

On the user front, users have to ensure that the free Silverlight plugin is downloaded and installed on their browser to play audio and animations.

Web developers can enjoy development on Silverlight because it supports video and audio files without need of a lot of programming. It permits to handle events such as start, end of videos from the web pages itself.

Q5. ★Which tools are required to develop Silverlight applications?
A5. Silverlight applications can be developed in a number of ways:

1. Use notepad to write the XAML code. After this, use the Silverlight SDK to compile the Silverlight application.

2. Microsoft Expression Studio - This tool is recommended for web developers who design rich graphic applications. It has got a lot of in built features for designing the UI such as color picker, selecting the fonts, etc. It is suggested not to use Microsoft Expression Studio in case the requirement is extremely programming intensive that requires usage of C# and VB.NET.

3. Microsoft Visual Studio - This is the most popular development environment by Microsoft. Prefer version 2010 or above. This can be used to develop Silverlight applications that require a lot of .NET programming. The Silverlight Development

Tools can be downloaded for free from the Microsoft website, in case these tools are not configured in Visual Studio.

Q6. ★ What is the Silverlight Runtime?
A6. The Silverlight Runtime is a plug-in by Microsoft for different browsers to allow Silverlight enabled applications run seamlessly on a user's system. In case the Silverlight runtime is not installed on a browser, the Silverlight application will not run. Developers may set the Silverlight tags such a way that your browser will automatically prompt the user to download and install the Silverlight plug in when your application is launched in the browser.

Installing the run time is a onetime operation on the client. Once installed, it will be automatically launched when any Silverlight application is loaded in the browser.

Q7. ★ What is the difference between Windows Presentation Foundation (WPF) and Silverlight?
A7. They have a separate XAML parser. Silverlight is mostly used to develop rich web based applications, whereas WPF is used for desktop based applications. However note that Silverlight can also be used to create desktop apps. WPF was introduced in .NET 3.0 Framework.

Also note that WPF supports advanced features of Windows Operating System such as 3D, hardware acceleration, and full document support. This is not supported in Silverlight.

Q8. ★ ★ What is the significance of a .xap file in Silverlight?
A8. A .xap file is basically a compiled Silverlight application. It is a kind of a zipped file that contains all the required files necessary for the Silverlight runtime to run the application.

The .xap file contains an application manifest (AppManifest.xaml) file and all the required DLLs which are required by the application to run. The .dll file has the same name as that of the application.

Q9. ★ ★ What is the significance of the AppManifest.xaml file?
A9. The AppManifest.xaml file is essentially comprised of the information about the .xap file such as the relevant .dll files. See the sample AppManifest.xaml file below:

```
<Deployment
    xmlns="http://schemas.microsoft.com/client/2007/deployment"
    xmlns:x="http://schemas.microsoft.com/winfx/2006/xaml"
    EntryPointAssembly="SilverlightApplication1"
    EntryPointType="SilverlightApplication1.App"
    RuntimeVersion="2.0.30226.2">
  <Deployment.Parts>
    <AssemblyPart x:Name="SilverlightApplication1" Source="SilverlightApplication1.dll" />
    <AssemblyPart x:Name="System.Windows.Controls" Source="System.Windows.Controls.dll" />
    <AssemblyPart x:Name="System.Windows.Controls.Extended"
Source="System.Windows.Controls.Extended.dll" />
  </Deployment.Parts>
</Deployment>
```

The AssemblyPart node specifies the assemblies inside the .xap file. The starting node has the EntryPointAssembly and EntryPointType attribute. The EntryPointAssembly attribute defines the main assembly of the application. Further, note that the EntryPointType attribute specifies the Class inside the assembly. The Deployment node has a RuntimeVersion attribute that specifies the version of Silverlight used to build the application.

Q10. ★What are the types of video files supported by Silverlight?
A10. The Silverlight platform supports MP3, Windows Media Audio format (wma, wmv7-9), and VC-1 formats.

Q11. ★What are the ways through which text may be displayed in Silverlight?
A11. The Silverlight platform supports displaying preformatted text in a static fashion; a text made up of glymph elements. It also supports dynamic text with the use of TextBlock. In case glyphs are used, the text location needs to be explicitly specified. On the other hand, if a TextBlock is used, a simple layout is supported.

Q12. ★★Which method can be used to figure out whether a Silverlight application is running inside a browser or outside a browser?
A12. The following methods may be useful to figure this out:

System.Windows.Application.Current.IsRunningOutOfBrowser()

System.AppDomain.CurrentDomain.IsRunningOutOfBrowser()

Q13. ★★What is the significance of the ClientBin folder?
A13. The ClientBin folder is basically used to keep the .xap file. Thought the .xap file may be kept anywhere, the ClientBin folder acts as the default storage location for the .xap file.

Q14. ★★What is Moonlight?
A14. Moonlight is an open source implementation of Silverlight, essentially for the Linux platform and other Unix based operating systems. Historically, during September 2007, Microsoft and Novell collaborated so that Microsoft could share its test suites for Silverlight and the distribute a Media Pack for Linux users that will contain licensed media codecs for video and audio. Later, Moonlight 2 was released in December 2009.

Q15. ★★What is RIA?
A15. RIA stands for Rich Internet Applications. These are rich internet applications comprising animations, layouts, video and audio capability and Ajax support.
Further, note that RIA is a library of client and server components that run on top of ADO.NET Data Services.

Q16. ★Can an application running on Silverlight be shown in Full-Screen mode?
A16. Yes, this is possible using the following command:

Application.Current.Host.Content.IsFullScreen = true;

Q17. ★What is Deep Zoom in Silverlight?

A17. Deep Zoom is a feature of Silverlight that allows zooming in and out of an application, without affecting the performance of the application.

Q18. ★★What is a Deep Zoom Composer in Silverlight?
A18. Deep zooming in Silverlight is done using a deep zoom composer, which helps developers in the process of creating high resolution images for panning and seamless zooming.

Q19. ★Can a Silverlight application be developed without the .NET Framework?
A19. Yes. The underlying fact is that if you use the Silverlight Framework version 4.0, this version already includes a compact version of .NET, and hence Silverlight can work independently.

Q20. ★★Which layout controls come with Silverlight?
A20. There are three main types of controls namely:
1. **Canvas** – This allows positioning the child elements according to the X, Y space.

2. **Grid** – This allows positioning the child elements in either rows or columns.

3. **StackPanel** – This allows positioning of child elements either horizontally or vertically.

Q21. ★How do you change the default page settings of a Silverlight page?
A21. This may be done by setting the RootVisual property in the Application_Startup event of the App.xaml file. The sample syntax is shown below:

```
Private void Application_Startup(object sender, StartupEventArgs e)
{
    this.RootVisual = new MainPage();
}
```

Q22. ★How is Ajax better than a Java applet?
A22. In general, Ajax based application runs faster than a Java applet, because Java applets load big sized libraries, where as in Ajax, code resides on the web server wherein only the required event in the user interface is posted back to the server.

CHAPTER 13 – Design Patterns

Q1. ★What is a Design Pattern?
A1. **Design Pattern** is a re-usable, high quality solution to a given requirement, task or recurring problem. Further, it does not comprise of a complete solution that may be instantly converted to a code component, rather it provides a framework for how to solve a problem.

In 1994, the release of the book Design Patterns, Elements of Reusable Object Oriented Software made design patterns popular.

Because design patterns consist of proven reusable architectural concepts, they are reliable and they speed up software development process.

Design Patterns are in a continuous phase of <u>evolution</u>, which means that they keep on getting better & better as they are tested against time, reliability and subjected to continuous improvements. Further, design patterns have evolved towards targeting specific domains. For example, windows-based banking applications are usually based on singleton patterns, e-commerce web applications are based on the MVC (Model-View-Controller) pattern.

Design Patterns are categorized into 3 types:

- ✓ Creational Patterns
- ✓ Structural Patterns
- ✓ Behavioral Patterns

Q2. ★What are Creational Design Patterns?
A2. The **Creational Design Patterns** focus on how objects are created and utilized in an application. They tackle the aspects of when and how objects are created, keeping in mind what's the best way these objects should be created.

Listed below are some of the commonly known Creational Design Patterns:

- ✓ Abstract Factory Pattern
- ✓ Factory Pattern
- ✓ Builder Pattern
- ✓ Lazy Pattern
- ✓ Prototype Pattern
- ✓ Singleton Pattern

Q3. ★★What's the difference between Abstract Factory Pattern and Factory Pattern?
A3. In an **abstract factory design**, a framework is provided for creating sub-components that inherit from a common component. In .NET, this is achieved by creating classes that implement a common interface or a set of interfaces, where the interface comprises of the generic method declarations that are passed on to the sub-components. Note that not just interfaces, but even abstract classes can provide the platform of creating an application based on the abstract factory pattern.

For example, say a class called CentralGovernmentRules is the abstract factory class, comprised of methods like ShouldHavePolice() and ShouldHaveCourts(). There may be several sub-classes like State1Rules, State2Rules etc. created that inheriting the class CentralGovernmentRules, and thus deriving its methods as well.

Note that the term "Factory" refers to the location in the code where the code is created.

A Factory Pattern is again an Object creation pattern. Here objects are created without knowing the class of the object. Sounds strange? Well, actually this means that the object is created by a method of the class, and not by the class's constructor. So basically the Factory Pattern is used wherever sub classes are given the privilege of instantiating a method that can create an object.

Q4. ★★Describe the Builder Design Pattern
A4. In a builder design pattern, an object creation process is separated from the object design construct. This is useful because the same method that deals with construction of the object can be used to construct different design constructs.

Q5. ★★What is the Lazy Design Pattern?
A5. The approach of the Lazy Design Pattern is not to create objects until a specific requirement matches, and when it matches, object creation is triggered. A simple example of this pattern is a Job Portal application. Say you register yourself in that site thus filling up the registration table, only when the registration table is filled, the other objects are created and invoked, that prompt you to fill in other details too, which will be saved in other tables.

Q6. ★★What is the Prototype Design Pattern?
A6. A prototype design pattern relies on creation of clones rather than objects. Here, we avoid using the keyword 'new' to prevent overheads.

Q7. ★★What is the Singleton Design Pattern?
A7. The **Singleton** design pattern is based on the concept of restricting the instantiation of a class to one object. Say one object needs to perform the role of a coordinator between various instances of the application that depend on a common object; we may design an application using a Singleton. Usage of Singleton patterns is common in Banking, Financial and Travel based applications where the singleton object consists of the network related information.

A singleton class may be used to instantiate an object of it, only if that object does not already exist. In case the object exists, a reference to the existing object is given. A singleton object has one global point of access to it.

An ASP.NET Web Farm is also based on the Singleton pattern. In a Web Farm, the web application resides on several web servers. The session state is handled by a Singleton object in the form of the aspnet_state.exe that interacts with the ASP.NET worker process running on each web server. Note that the worker process is the aspnet_wp.exe process. Imagine one of the web servers shutting down; the singleton object aspnet_state.exe still maintains the session state information across all web servers in the web farm.

In .NET, in order to create a singleton, a class is created with a private constructor, and a "static readonly" variable as the member that behaves as the instance.

Q8. ★★What are Structural Design Patterns?

A8. A structural design pattern establishes a relationship between entities. This makes it easier for different components of an application to interact with each other. Following are some of the commonly known structural patterns:

✓ **Adapter Pattern** - Interfaces of classes vary depending on the requirement.
✓ **Bridge Pattern** - Class level abstraction is separated from its implementation.
✓ **Composite Pattern** - Individual objects & a group of objects are treated similarly in this approach.
✓ **Decorator Pattern** - Functionality is assigned to an object. Facade Pattern - A common interface is created for a group of interfaces sharing a similarity. Flyweight Pattern - The concept of sharing a group of small sized objects.
✓ **Proxy Pattern** - When an object is complex and needs to be shared, its copies are made. These copies are called the proxy objects.

Q9. ★What are the different types of Proxy Patterns?

A9. The following are the different types of Proxy Patterns.

✓ **Remote Proxy** - A reference is given to a different object in a different memory location. This may be on a different or a same machine.
✓ **Virtual Proxy** - This kind of object is created only & only when really required because of its memory usage.
✓ **Cache Proxy** - An object that behaves as a temporary storage so that multiple applications may use it. For example, in ASP.NET when a page or a user control contains the OutputCache directive, that page/control is cached for some time on the ASP.NET web server.

Q10. ★★What is a behavioral design pattern?

A10. Behavioral design patterns focus on improving the communication between different objects. Following are different types of behavioral patterns:

✓ **Chain Or Responsibilities Pattern** - In this pattern, objects communicate with each other depending on logical decisions made by a class.
✓ **Command Pattern** - In this pattern, objects encapsulate methods and the parameters passed to them.
✓ **Observer Pattern** - Objects are created depending on events results, for which there are event handlers created.

Q11. ★★What is the MVC Pattern (Model View Controller Pattern)?

A11. The MVC Pattern (Model View Controller Pattern) is based on the concept of designing an application by dividing its functionalities into 3 layers. It's like a triad of components. The Model component contains the business logic, or the other set of re-usable classes like classes pertaining to data access, custom control classes, application configuration classes etc. The Controller component interacts with the Model whenever required. The control contains events and methods inside it, which are raised from the UI which is the View component.

Consider an ASP.NET web application. Here, all aspx, ascx, master pages represent the View.

The code behind files (such as aspx.cs, master.cs, ascx.cs) represents the Controller.

The classes contained in the App_Code folder, or rather any other class project being referenced from this application represent the Model component.

Advantages:

- ✓ Business logic can be easily modified, without affecting or any need to make changes in the UI.
- ✓ Any cosmetic change in the UI does not affect any other component.

Q12. ★What is the Gang of Four Design Pattern?
A12. The history of all design patterns used in modern day applications derive from the Gang of Four (GoF) Pattern. Gang of Four patterns are categorized into 3 types:

- ✓ **Creational**
- ✓ **Structural**
- ✓ **Behavioral**

The term "Gang of Four" *(or "GoF" in acronym)* is used to refer to the four authors of the book **Design Patterns: Elements of Reusable Object-Oriented Software**. The authors are Erich Gamma, Ralph Johnson, Richard Helm and John Vlissides.

Q13. ★When should design patterns be used?
A13. While developing software applications, sound knowledge of industry proven design patterns make the development journey easy and successful. Whenever a requirement is recurring, a suitable design pattern should be identified. Usage of optimal design patterns enhances performance of the application. Though there are some caveats. Make sure that there are no overheads imposed on a simple requirement, which means that design patterns should not be unnecessarily be used.

Q14. ★How many design patterns can be created in .NET?
A14. As many as one can think! Design patterns are not technology specific; rather their foundation relies on the concept of reusability, object creation and communication. Design patterns can be created in any language.

Q15. ★★Describe the Ajax Design Pattern.
A15. In an Ajax Design Pattern, partial postbacks are triggered asynchronously to a web server for getting live data. A web application would not flicker here, and the web site user would not even come to know that a request is being sent to the web server for live data.

Such a design pattern is used in applications like Stock Market Websites to get live quotes, News Websites for live news, Sports websites for live scores etc.

Q15. ★★What is a delegate pattern?
A15. The delegation pattern is a pattern where in an object is made to perform a task on behalf of another object. The object to which the task is assigned is referred to as the helper object. A helper object is also called the delegate object. The object whose task is being performed is called the delegator.

Q16. ★★★What is a momento pattern?
A16. A momento pattern allows an object to get back to its original state. This pattern is utilized by two objects namely the originator and the caretaker. The originator object has an internal state. The caretaker acts responsibly by taking care of the originator. The caretaker actually performs an action on the originator, and makes sure that it converts back the originator object to its original state. So basically the caretaker maintains a momento of the originator in the form of a momento object.

CHAPTER 14 – MVC

Q1. ★★Is MVC a framework or a design pattern? What is MVC?
A1. Both. Read on:

Model View Controller (MVC) is a software design pattern that separates the application logic (business logic) from the user interface (the presentation layer) and the backend. This facilitates a loosely coupled setup of the code, and allows independent development, testing and maintenance of each layer. An application built on the MVC design pattern separates different aspects of the application (input logic, business logic and UI logic).

MVC is a mature design pattern and comes in various styles. However, the control flow is generic, as described below.

- ✓ End users have a way to interact with the user interface (such as a right click)
- ✓ The inputs are handled by a controller by interacting with the user interface, this usually happens through a known handler or callback; the event is then converted back to a corresponding action
- ✓ The model is informed by the controller about the action, and the model then takes care of the interaction with the database.
- ✓ The UI is then dynamically set as a result of a query which is sent by the view to the model
- ✓ When another user event takes place, the lifecycle starts again

The idea behind the MVC design pattern is to decouple models and views, and to reduce the complexity in architectural design and to maximize maintainability and flexibility of the code.

Further, an implementation of MVC has been done in ASP.NET. This is called the **ASP.NET MVC Framework**. This framework implements the Model View Controller design pattern. It permits developers to create applications comprised of three roles namely Model, View and Controller. The model represents the state of an aspect of an application. This role takes care of the interaction with the database. Generally, the state of the application is saved in a table in the database. The controller handles the interactions and ensures that the model is updated in order to output the changed state of the application. It then transfers information back to the view. The view takes the inputs from the controller and accordingly refreshes the user interface.

The first version of the ASP.NET MVC framework is called the ASP.NET MVC CTP. This was launched in December 2007. The latest version of ASP.NET MVC framework is the ASP.NET MVC 4.0 Framework.

Q2. ★How to create an MVC project in ASP.NET MVC?
A2. The following steps may be carried out to create an ASP.NET MVC project:

1. On the File menu, click on New Project. The New Project Dialog box will be displayed.
2. In the upper right corner, click on .NET Framework 4.0
3. Under Project Types, select either Visual Basic or C#. Next, click Web.
4. Under Visual Studio installed templates, select ASP.NET MVC 4 Web Application.
5. In the Name box, enter the name of your project.
6. Specify a location for the project.
7. In case you want a different name for the Solution, specify it in the box meant for Solution.
8. Select Create directory for solution.
9. Click on OK.

After this, you will see the Create Unit Test Project dialog box.

Q3. ★Can you create an MVC Unit Test Project in Visual Studio Standard?
A3. No. Also note that you can't create an MVC Unit Test Project in Visual Studio Express too. It can be created in Visual Studio Professional and Visual Studio Enterprise versions.

Q4. ★★What is an asynchronous controller in ASP.NET MVC?
A4. AsyncController is a class that empowers developers to write asynchronous action methods. Developers may use asynchronous action methods for long duration processes. This helps the web server optimize its performance by not using extra resources when a request is being processed. The AsyncController class is mainly used in web service calls that take a long time.

Q5. ★★★How does a thread pool process requests? What is thread starvation? How are asynchronous requests processed?
A5. The .NET Framework manages a pool of threads which are used to serve the requests in ASP.NET. Whenever a request comes in to a web server, a thread is allocated to process the request. In case the request is processed synchronously, this thread gets blocked. In a pool, several locked threads can handle individual requests. However, due to limitation of resources, all available threads might get blocked at some point of time. This situation is termed as **thread starvation**.

An asynchronous request handling process handles multiple requests. As this is an asynchronous approach, the queuing of requests is prevented.

The following steps take place when an asynchronous action happens:

✓ A thread in the web server is first of all identified. This thread is referred to as the **worker thread**. This worker thread processes the asynchronous request.

✓ As soon as it gets a request, the worker thread is again made available to the thread pool in order to handle a new web request.
✓ In parallel, the asynchronous process keeps going on. When it completes, ASP.NET is notified.
✓ For each subsequent request of the application, the web server is allocated a worker thread from the thread pool. This may be a separate thread from the thread that initially started the asynchronous operation.

Q6. ★Point out some advantages of the MVC Framework.
A6. The following are some advantages of the MVC Framework.

✓ MVC facilitates a great support for test-driven development (TDD).
✓ MVC uses the Front Controller pattern to processes Web application requests using a solitary controller. This empowers developers to develop systems that have a lot of internal information routing.
✓ The MVC framework allows simpler management of complex applications by slicing them into the model, the view, and the controller.
✓ MVC works without a viewstate. This ensures that developers have complete control on the application.

Q7. ★★Why is it suggested not to use controls such as GridView, Repeater and DataList with the ASP.NET MVC Framework?
A7. ASP.NET MVC Framework does not support viewstate. But because GridView, Repeater and DataList need a ViewState to function properly, it is not advised to use these controls in the ASP.NET MVC Framework.

Q8. ★★Which are the Validation Helpers available in ASP.NET MVC?
A8. There are two validation helpers available in ASP.NET:

✓ Html.ValidationMessage()
✓ Html.ValidationSummary()

Q9. ★★How to use validation helpers in ASP.NET MVC?
A9. Validation Helpers are used in a view in order to show validation error messages. The **Html.ValidationMessage()** and Html.ValidationSummary() helpers are used in the Edit and Create views that are generated automatically by the ASP.NET MVC. In order to create a view, the following steps may be carried out:

1. Right-click on the Create() action in the Product controller and then select the menu option Add View.
2. In the Add View dialog, check the checkbox labeled Create a strongly-typed view.
3. From the View data class dropdown list, select the Product class.
4. Next, from the View content dropdown list, select Create.
5. Lastly, click the Add button.

Q10. ★What is Razor?
A10. Razor is basically a new syntax for writing ASP.NET pages that facilitates creating a view. It is processed server-side. It is free and developed by Microsoft. It can be used with C# and VB.NET. Further, it promotes writing code in the ASP.NET MVC Framework.

Q11. ★★How to implement a Gridview in ASP.NET MVC?

A11.There is a built-in WebGrid Helper in ASP.NET MVC that helps to create this. This WebGrid helper was introduced in MVC 3. Using a simple command, **@grid.getHtml()** can be used to return a populated table with sorting, paging, and GridView lines with alternate lines. The following is a code example that shows how a WebGrid reads data from a database:

```
@{
    var db = Database.Open("StockExchange") ;
    var selectQueryString = "SELECT * FROM Nifty ORDER BY Id";
    var data = db.Query(selectQueryString);
    var grid = new WebGrid(data);
}
```

Further, on the HTML page, the following may be used:

```
<div id="grid"> @grid.GetHtml() </div>
```

Q12. ★★How to create a view for multiple models?

A12. A view can have only one model. However, you can create a class that has two or more models, and then make your view point to that class. In fact you can add any number of models to that class.

Q13. ★What are the other popular MVC Frameworks besides the ASP.NET MVC Framework?

A13. Struts, Spring MVC, Zend, Aranea, Cocoon, CodeCharge Studio, JSF, Makumba web development framework, Oracle Application Framework, PureMVC, Sling, Stripes, Tapestry, Wavemaker, Wicket, and Web Dynpro Java.

Q14. ★What is NerdDinner?

A14. NerdDinner is a freely available application built using ASP.NET MVC 2.0. It allows easy learning of the ASP.NET MVC Framework by building an application side by side in order to learn the framework. You may refer to www.nerddinner.com to explore and learn through this approach. The application allows people to find and organize dinners online.

Q15. ★★How are CSRF attacks avoided in ASP.NET MVC Framework?

A15. ASP.NET Framework promotes the usage of anti-forgery helpers to avoid CSRF attacks. This is done by using HTML helpers that are used in a form that renders internal inputs. Further, the attributes are applied to the controller's action to carry out the necessary protection required.

CHAPTER 15 – Advanced Interview Questions

Q1. ★★How are Web Services used in ASP.NET? What is a web service?
A1. A Web Service is a method available over the web, either securely or directly. In order to use a web service in ASP.NET, we need to create a web service and add a web reference into ASP.NET.

There are two ways for calling a web service, first is the synchronous approach, the other is the asynchronous approach.

Synchronous approach invoking a web service:

Example (C#):

```
TheWebServiceName.Service obj = new TheWebServiceName.Service();
obj.WebServiceMethod();
```

Asynchronous approach for invoking a web service:

```
TheWebServiceName.Service obj = new TheWebServiceName.Service();
System.AsyncCallback cb = new AsyncCallback(showmsg);
obj.BeginWebServiceMethod(cb, someWS);
void showmsg(IAsyncResult o)
{
    TheWebServiceName.Service someWS = (TheWebServiceName.Service)ar.AsyncState;
    Response.Write(obj.EndWebServiceMethod(o));
}
```

Q2. ★★What is the difference between a Web Application project and a Website project?
A2. In a **website project** model, the website's structure makes use of a directory structure in order to define the contents of the project. In this model, there isn't any project file, and all files in the directory are part of the project.

On the other hand, in a **Web application project**, the files which are explicitly referenced in the solution's project file are the only ones that are part of the project. These files are showed in the **Solution Explorer**, and these are the only files that are compiled during a build.

Q3. ★★What is a postback? How do ASP.NET controls trigger a postback?
A3. First of all, note that it is worth knowing in detail about these two interfaces - **IPostBackEventHandler** and **IPostBackDataHandler**.

The IPostBackEventHandler defines the methods that ASP.NET server controls must implement to handle any postback event. Invoking functions such as **Page.GetPostBackEventReference** and **Page.GetPostBackClientHyperlink** allows ASP.Net to render the JavaScript Function **__doPostBack()**, which submits the form with postback. To check how to perform postbacks for custom events, you may check the following sample. First, define the onmouseover event on the client side to do the JavaScript function __doPostBack which can do postback to Code Behind.

```
ImageButtonX.Attributes.Add("onmouseover",
Page.GetPostBackClientHyperlink(ImageButtonX,"onmouseover"));
```

See below how the Page_Load retrieves the __doPostBack().

```
protected void Page_Load(object sender, EventArgs e)
{
    if (Request.Params["__EVENTTARGET"] != null)
    {
        string target = Request.Params["__EVENTTARGET"].ToString();
        string passedArgument = Request.Params["__EVENTARGUMENT"].ToString();
        if (target == "ImageButtonX" && passedArgument == "onmouseover")
        {
            // your code goes here
        }
    }
}
```

The Page.**GetPostBackClientHyperlink** will register the __doPostBack JavaScript function at the client to execute the __doPostBack('ImageButtonX','onmouseover'). This happens when the 'onmouseover' client side event of the ImageButtonX fires.

Q4. ★★How to dynamically build an ASP.NET Server Side Table?
A4. In ASP.NET, a server side table has a 'runat="server" attribute, where as a client side table does not have runat="server" attribute.

- ✓ We can build an ASP.NET Server Side Table in server side code through the code behind.
- ✓ We can build a Client Side Table using JavaScript.

Q5. ★★★How can you zip a file or a folder in .NET?
A5. Zipping can be achieved by using the java.util.zip.ZipFile, ICSharpCode.SharpZipLib.Zip or any other library *(assembly)* that allows zipping.

You may try the SharpZipLib that you can easily google out and then download.

> **Note**: There is a new GZipStream class introduced in .Net Framework 2.0 under **System.IO.Compression**. It is for GZip, which uses RFC1952, making it different from Zip.

Q6. ★★★How do we check whether a user is online or offline?
A6. Many developers tend to use the '**Session_End**' event to mark a user as 'Offline', but this may not be a good idea, because there are no one-to-one mappings between an ASP.Net session and a user. For example if a user opens two separate instances of Internet Explorer (e.g. two separate IE processes) on his/her workstation, he/she can have two ASP.Net sessions open. The 'Session_End' event of one of the session does not necessarily mean that the user is offline; he/she can still be using the website.
It is suggested using the last visiting time as the ideal approach.

> **TIP**: The 'Session_End' event is only available in the 'InProc' session mode. If you are trying to store session states in the State Server or SQL Server, 'Session_End' event, it will never fire.

Membership helps create the user database and there is a convenient approach to get it via **Membership.GetUser(string userName).IsOnline**.

If we don't use Membership, we can use the method below which uses the same principle in Membership:

- ✓ In the application, we can define a global dictionary **membershipDictionary** to store the information about users online and offline.
- ✓ Use an AJAX Timer (or simple XmlHttpRequest at the client side JavaScript) in the pages to update the LastVisitTime of the user and store it into membershipDictionary at intervals.
- ✓ At regular intervals, visit the dictionary membershipDictionary to filter out the idle users (who have not visited the page for a long time) and also retrieve information on how many users are still online. Regular maintenance can be done in a separate thread or a server-based timer. Please also be aware of thread synchronization issues.

Q7, ★★★Is there a way to insert a special non-ASCII characters into a database?

A7. When we try to insert a special non-ASCII characters into a database, such as 'Kookaboorâ€™s', we find that they can't be inserted, by using "INSERT INTO table VALUES(1,'Kookaboorâ€™s')", only "Kookaboora€?s" can be inserted.

However, we can insert the value as parameter into the database. See the code below.

Example (C#):

```
InsertCon.Open();
SqlCommand InsertCmd = new SqlCommand("INSERT INTO table VALUES (1,@name)", InsertCon);
InsertCmd.Parameters.Add(new SqlParameter("@name", SqlDbType.NVarChar,200));
InsertCmd.Parameters["@name"].Value = TextBox1.Text; //Assume the input is validated and legal.
InsertCmd.ExecuteNonQuery();
InsertCon.Close();
```

If we use this approach, we may prevent potential SQL injection attacks.

Q8. ★★What is the difference between <%# %> and <%= %> symbols?

A8. The <%# %> is used for data binding while <%= %> is used to output the result of an expression. The expression inside <%# %> will be executed only when we call the page's or control's DataBind method. The expression inside <%= %> will be executed and displayed when it appears on the page.

Q9. ★★★Is it possible to step into a DLL's source code from ASP.NET application while debugging?

A9. Firstly, if you are using the 'Release' build of the modules, please try building the modules or application under the 'Debug' build.

If the debugger cannot load the DLL's **.PDB** file, we also cannot use the source code. **The PDB files are debug symbols** that are generated with the modules (EXE/DLL). They hold the necessary information for source code level debugging. The debugger will not load a PDB that does not match the binary being debugged. You can check if the debugger loads this PDB file by using the following steps:

- ✓ Start debugging.
- ✓ Click 'Debug' menu and then select 'Windows' to enter the 'Modules' window.
- ✓ Locate your DLL module to see if the PDB file is loaded. If the PDB file is not loaded, you can load it manually by right clicking the DLL module and then select 'Load Symbols' option).

Q10. ★★★Why is it that the breakpoint doesn't work sometimes during debugging?
A10. There could be different reasons why this happens:

1. Matching symbols cannot be found without symbols, breakpoints cannot be mapped from source code to machine code while it is being executed.
2. The source code you have opened inside Visual Studio does not match the build of the executable code you're trying to debug. If you are aware of this but want the debugger to attempt to set the breakpoint anyway, you can do one of following:
Right click on the breakpoint and choose 'Location...' Then check the 'Allow the source code to be different from the original version' checkbox.
Next, turn off the source code verification. Go to the menu Tools → **Options** → **Debugging** → **General** and uncheck 'Require source files to exactly match the original version'.
3. It may be possible that the component or program you have set the breakpoint to, have not been loaded into the memory yet. When a DLL or component is loaded to your program, the debugger is informed and will attempt to bind the breakpoint so that it can be hit.

Q11. ★★★How to improve the performance of ASP.NET pages?
A11. We can improve the ASP.NET application performance by the following ways:

- ✓ Use Page.IsPostBack
- ✓ Use SQL Server Stored Procedures for Data Access, as they are precompiled
- ✓ Use the HttpServerUtility.Transfer method
- ✓ Save View State Only When Necessary.
- ✓ Do not rely on Exceptions.
- ✓ Restrict Use of Session State.
- ✓ Limit ASP.NET Server Controls as their viewstate eat a lot of memory
- ✓ Precompile the applications
- ✓ Use ASP.NET Caching
- ✓ Make sure that backend performance is tuned

Q12. ★★What is the character '~' used for in ASP.NET?
A12. The character tilde (~) in the ASP.NET paths points to the root of the web application.

Web developers are familiar with using relative paths for all links, including hyperlinks, images and style sheets to be able to move around web pages collectively.

In ASP.NET, while using user controls, the relative paths can be tough and confusing to use. The typical solution to this is to use web root absolute paths instead, such as '~/pageUc.ascx', resulting in the hard-coded sub-directories that are common on ASP.NET sites.

The correct solution to this problem is to use app-relative paths instead, which ASP.NET beautifully makes possible through the use of the tilde (~) prefix. Instead of the <a href="/UC/Page.aspx">, use <a id="P1" href="~/Page.aspx" runat="server">. The same ~ notation works for images also, as long as you add runat="server". There is also a ResolveUrl method that allows you to use ~ in your own code, which is one possible way to get stylesheet paths app-relative.

Q13. ★★What is the difference between 'System.Net.Mail' and 'System.Web.Mail'?

A13. The **System.Web.Mail** and the **System.Net.Mail** are both built-in libraries provided by Microsoft in the .NET framework. System.Web.Mail is supported by all versions of .Net Frameworks at the moment. However, System.Web.Mail is obsolete since .Net 2.0 could be removed from the class library in the future. In .Net 2.0, the new 'System.Net.Mail' namespace has been included. It is suggested against 'System.Web.Mail', if you are developing applications targeting the .Net 2.0 framework and later.

Q14. ★★★How to get the index of a row that contains the clicked control in a GridView?

A14. This may be done by using the property **CommandName** and the event **RowCommand** of the GridView control.

In order to get the index of a row that contains the clicking control in GridView, we may try the method below.

1. First of all, define the property CommandName in an ImageButton control: CommandName="display"

```
<asp:TemplateField>
<ItemTemplate>
<asp:ImageButton ID="ImageButton1" runat="server" ImageUrl='<%# Eval("ImageUrl",
"~/images/stock/{0}") %>' Height="120px"
    CommandName="display" Width="160px"/>
</ItemTemplate>
</asp:TemplateField>
```

2. In the event **RowDataBound**, pass the row index to the ImageButton CommandArgument, as follows:

```
protected void GridView1_RowDataBound(object sender, GridViewRowEventArgs e)
{
  if (e.Row.RowType == DataControlRowType.DataRow)
  {
    ImageButton imgBut = ((ImageButton)e.Row.Cells[1].Controls[1]);
    imgBut.CommandArgument = e.Row.RowIndex.ToString();
  }
}
```

3. Next, use the **RowCommand** event to execute the click event of the ImageButton, so that you can get the index.

Q15 ★★★How to refresh a page in another page?
A15. In the example below, after the user closes the child page, the parent page will be refreshed.

Parent page: (*use window.open to open the popup page*)

```
<asp:Button ID="Button1" OnClientClick="javascript:window.open('Popup.aspx');" runat="server"
Text="Button" />
```

Popup.aspx: (After clicking the Button1, it will submit the change and refresh the parent page.)

```
protected void Button1_Click(object sender, EventArgs e)
{
    if (IsChanged())//the user made a change
    {
        Page.ClientScript.RegisterStartupScript(this.GetType(),            "refresh",          "
window.opener.location.reload(); ", true);
        Page.ClientScript.RegisterStartupScript(this.GetType(), "close", "window.close();", true);
    }
}
```

Q16. ★★★How to display dynamic ToolTips for controls?
A16. Some controls have the property '**ToolTip**' which can display the details when a mouse cursor moves over.

However, when we want to display dynamic tooltips for every cell in a GridView or display dynamic tooltips of every specific day in Calendar, the property 'ToolTip' is not sufficient and something innovative can accomplish this.

In order to implement the dynamic tooltips for the controls, we can use the **Control.Attributes.Add** and tooltips JavaScript function to deploy respective tooltip for every control.

Display the dynamical tooltips of every cell in GridView:

You may download wz_tooltip.zip from the link below:
http://www.walterzorn.com/tooltip/tooltip e.htm   (*This URL may not remain forever*)

You can add the 'onmouseover' event to every cell to display tooltips via 'Attributes.Add' in GridViewX_RowDataBound.

Q17. ★★★What is a dependency injection?
A17. It is a design pattern, the purpose of which is to reduce the dependency between software components in an application or system. It is similar to the factory pattern. When a dependency injection pattern is used, an object does not need to be aware of what the other part of the system is all about. Rather, the developer injects the required system components in advance along with a ruleset that will perform in a particular fashion.

A dependency injection pattern is composed of three things:
- ✓ A dependency consumer
- ✓ A definition of the service dependency

✓ An injector

Q18. ★★What is the difference between optimistic locking and pessimistic locking?

A18. **Locking** is a concept implemented in order to guard records that will be accessed by multiple users so that concurrency errors can be avoided. It prevents access through some technique and protects a record when a user is doing an update.

Optimistic locking is better to use when the chances of an update conflict is low. This is usually the scene when the routine activity is happening by adding a record. **Pessimistic locking** is used when the chances of a conflict is high.

Pessimistic locking guesses contention for the same record thereby prevents users from selecting a record for editing whenever the other user has done it beforehand. This is usually carried out by banking upon the database itself. Most relational databases utilize this method. However, each database may use a different approach for the way locking is done. For example, the SQL Server 2000 locks single rows, whereas others may lock the entire page or table containing the record to be changed. One of the drawbacks is that this type of locking demands that you remain connected to the database all the time.

Optimistic locking facilitates multiple users to access the same record for edits, counting on minimal conflicts over data. The locking occurs after the user tries to save changes on someone else's actions. The program logic checks to see if the record has been changed since the time you opened it. If it has changed, then an error is thrown and the update is rolled back. On the other hand, if no changes are detected, then the record is saved.

Q19. ★★What is cyclomatic complexity?

A19. Cyclomatic complexity is a metric in computer science that is used to measure the complexity of a computer program. It directly measures the count of the linearly independent paths in the source code. It is calculated by using a graph that depicts the control flow of a program. The nodes in the graph map to the command lines in the program. The stardard equation for cyclomatic complexity is:

$$CC = E - N + P$$

Where
CC = Cyclomatic Complexity
E = Number of edges of the graph
N = Number of nodes of the graph
P = Number of connected components

Q20. ★★What is a contract in WCF?

A20. WCF stands for Windows Communication Foundation. In WCF, all the services expose something called as a contract. A contract serves as a platform neutral way of showcasing what the services are being offered. This signifies what are the types of services that can be performed on the service by the client. Essentially, there are two types of service contracts:

- ✓ **ServiceContract** - This is the attribute used to define the Interface.
- ✓ **OperationContract** – This is the attribute used to define the method(s) inside Interface.

Example (C#):

```
[ServiceContract]
interface ITheContract
{
  [OperationContract]
  string TheMethod( );
}
class TheService : ITheContract
{
  public string TheMethod( )
  {
    return "Shoot the next question please";
  }

}
```

Q21. ★★How can you pass data to a user control?

A21: User controls may be comprised of several server side controls. In some scenarios, developers may need to set the properties of the internal controls from the outer page. The following may be carried out:

Say the user control's code behind file is uc.ascx.cs, open this file and then add a public method or property that the page would invoke.

Example (VB.NET):

```
Public Sub SetTheLabelText(ByVal val As String)
        Label1.Text = val
End Sub.
```

Now in the page's code behind file, declare a reference to the user control.

Protected WithEvents TheControl As TheUserControl

Next, the user control's custom method may be invoked from within the page.

TheControl.SetTheLabelText("That was an easy interview")

CHAPTER 16 – Rapid Fire Interview Questions

Q1. ★Which method is invoked on the DataAdapter control in order to load data in the dataset?
A1. The DataAdaptor's **Fill()** method is used to do this.

Q2. ★What is the most common use of a private constructor?
A2. A private constructor may be used to prevent the creation of an instance for a class.

Q3. ★★Give one use of a Singleton pattern.
A3. Use it to ensure that only one instance of a class exists.

Q4. ★★When do we use a DOM parser and when do we use a SAX parser?
A4. The DOM Approach is useful for small documents in which the program needs to process a large portion of the document whereas the SAX approach is useful for large documents in which the program only needs to process a small portion of the document.

Q5. ★Expand MVC.
A5. Model – View – Controller. It is a design pattern. Several programming frameworks have been built using this pattern.

Q6. ★What is the file extension for a web handler?
A6. .ashx

Q7. ★What is an ActiveX Data Object *(ADO)*?
A7. Microsoft ActiveX Data Objects *(ADO)* is a collection of Component Object Model objects for accessing different types of data sources.

Q8. ★What is an Active Server Page (ASP)?
A8. Active Server Page is Microsoft's Server side script engine for creating dynamic web pages.

Q9. ★What is SSIS used for?
A9. SSIS i.e. SQL Server Integration Services is an SQL technology by Microsoft, used for easily integrating with enterprise platforms with different types of data sources. The SSIS is used to build a bundled logic in the form of a package. The packages may be used to copy or download data files, update huge databases such as data warehouses, send emails and updates, and interact with other packages to solve business needs.

Q10. ★What is VSTS?
A10. VSTS stands for Visual Studio Team Suite. It is an extended version of Visual Studio. VSTS is comprised of collaboration and development tools to archive software development requirements.

Q11. ★★When do you get invalid cast exceptions, during compile time or during runtime?
A11. During runtime.

Q12. ★★★What is the use of the peek() method of the TextReader class?
A12. The peek() method of the TextReader class returns the next character with reference to the current character, without actually moving to the next character.

In case -1 is returned, it means that the reference is currently at the last character of the string.

Q13. ★★What is the difference between the .Show() method and the .ShowDialog() method of the UserMessageDialog object?

A13. When the **.Show()** method is used, the user can navigate between the dialog window and the main form behind the dialog window. On the other hand, the **ShowDialog()** method works in modal mode, which means the dialog window has to be closed before the user can navigate to the main form behind the dialog window.

Q14. ★What is a DataColumn?

A14. A DataColumn object represents a single column in a **DataTable** object.

Q15. ★What is the use of the System.Data.SqlTypes namespace?

A15. The System.Data.SqlTypes namespace comprises of native data types used by Microsoft SQL Server. These data types are optimized on the performance front for use with an SQL server.

Q16. ★★When a custom type is placed in the HttpSessionState object, which attribute is mandatory?

A16. It is important to use the [Serializable] attribute with the custom type being put in the HttpSessionState object.

Q17. ★In which version of ASP.NET was the DataGridView control introduced?

A17. The DataGridView control was introduced in ASP.NET 2.0.

Q18. ★What is the wsdl.exe used for?

A18. The wsdl.exe is a command line tool used to carry out the following activities:
- ✓ It is used to create a server side file that acts as a bucket for the implementation of a web service
- ✓ It is used to create a client side file that acts as a proxy to a remote XML web service

Q19. ★★Which event of the global.asax file is called when the application is run for the first time?

A19. The **Application_Start()** method. Note that this method runs only once in a lifetime of an application. If the application restarts (say the web server reboots), it will be called again.

Q20. ★What is the default value of the AutoPostBack property of an ASP.NET control, true or false?

A20. The default value is false.

Q21. ★In ASP.NET, which attribute of the Page directive can be used to automatically invoke the page load and unload events, whenever they take place?

A21. The **AutoEventWireUp** attribute can be set to 'true' to ensure that the page load and unload events are called, whenever these events take place. In case you set this value to false, the code inside the Page_Load and Page_Unload event blocks won't run.

Q22. ★What is WSDL?

A22. WSDL stands for Web Service Description Language. It is an XML based language for describing web services.

Q23. ★What is WML?

A23. WML stands for Wireless Markup Language. This is a content format for those devices that use Wireless Application Protocol.

Q24. ★For what purpose is the Sn.exe tool used?

A24. The Sn.exe tool is used to create strongly named assemblies.

Q25. ★What is RCW?

A25. RCW stands for Runtime Callable Wrapper. This component is used when a .NET component needs to be converted to a COM component.

Q26. ★★What is the size of a GUID?

A26. A Global Unique Identifier (GUID) is 128 bits (16 bytes).

Q27. ★★★What is CAO?

A27. CAO stands for client activated object. These are objects created on the server upon the client's request. This is used in remoting.

Q28. ★What is CIL?

A28. CIL stands for Common Intermediate Language. It is a low level human readable language implementation of CLI. All .NET languages convert code into CIL when compiled.

Q29. ★What is a HashTable object?

A29. A HashTable object contains a collection of paired items, where one item in the pair is a numerical key. This object implements the following interfaces – Idictionary, ICollection, IEnumerable and IClonable.

Q30. ★★Which method of a Queue object is used to add an item to the end of a queue?

A30. The Enqueue() method is used to add an item to the end of a queue. The Dequeue() method is used to remove an item from the beginning of a queue object.

Q31. ★What is a COM object?

A31. COM stands for Component Object Model. It is a reusable software component, built using legacy platforms by Microsoft. The tribe of COM components includes COM+, Distributed COM (DCOM) and ActiveX controls.

Q32. ★What is CTS?

A32. CTS stands for Common Type Specification. It is the core of .NET Framework's cross language integration, type safety, and high-performance code execution. It defines a common set of types that can be used with many different language syntaxes. Each language (C#, VB.NET, Managed C++, and so on) is free to define any syntax it wishes, but if that language is built on the CLR, it will use at least some of the types defined by the CTS.

Q33. ★What is Windows Cardspace?

A33. Windows Cardspace also referred to as WC was released with the .NET Framework 3.0. It enables users to store digital identities of a person, and a

---

provision to a unified interface for choosing the identity of a particular transaction, such as logging into a website.

Q34. ★What is Workflow Foundation?
A34. Workflow Foundation is also referred to as WF *(Not WWF)*. This was released with the .NET Framework 3.0. It is used for defining, executing and managing reusable workflows.

Q35. ★★What is a Well Known Object (WKO)?
A35. It is a MarshallByReference type whose lifetime is controlled by the server's application domain.

Q36. ★What is WPF?
A36. WPF stands for Windows Presentation Foundation. It was launched with the .NET 3.0 Framework. It is mainly the graphical sub system of the .NET Framework and promotes creation of graphics.

Q37. ★What is a .sln file?
A37. A .sln file contains the Visual Studio solution. It organizes projects, project items and solution items into this file by providing references to these resources, wherever they exist on the storage media.

Q38. ★★What is a .suo file?
A38. It is the Solution User Options file that records all the options that you associate with the solution. Basically it stores all the solution related settings that you have made.

Q39. ★★★How to play a song in a Windows based application using .NET?
A39. Use the class System.Media.SoundPlayer. See the code snippet below:

Example (VB.NET):

```
Private PlaySound As New System.Media.SoundPlayer
Public Sub PlaySoundFile(ByVal SoundPath As String)
        PlaySound .SoundLocation = SoundPath
        PlaySound .Load()
        PlaySound .Play()
End Sub
```

Q40. ★★How to dynamically register and invoke javascript from C#?
A40. Use the method ClientScript.RegisterClientScriptBlock. Note that there was an older method too called as Page.RegisterClientScriptBlock, but now this is deprecated.

Example (C#):

```
ClientScript.RegisterClientScriptBlock(typeof(Page), "theScript", "alert('Cracking interviews is now a cakewalk')", true);
```

Q41. ★What is ILDASM?
A41. **ILDASM** - The contents of an assembly may be viewed using the ILDASM tool that comes with the .NET SDK and with Visual Studio.NET. The ildasm.exe tool may also be used in the command line compiler. ILDASM basically stands for Intermediate Language Disassembler.

Q42. ★What's the advantage of using System.Text.StringBuilder over System.String?
A42. StringBuilder is more efficient in the cases, where a lot of manipulation is done to the text. Strings are immutable, so each time it's being operated on, a new instance is created. 144

Q43. ★Where can you you host WCF services?
A43. There are three popular ways of hosting WCF services.

- ✓ IIS
- ✓ Self Hosting
- ✓ WAS (Windows Activation Service)

Q44. ★★What is new in the ASP.NET 4.0's web.config file?
A44. This web.config file is much smaller and cleaner. Instead of containing all the configuration settings, it rather points to .NET Framework to be picked for compiling the code through the compilation section inside the system.web section.

Q45. ★★What is a control state in ASP.NET?
A45. The concept of control state was introduced in ASP.NET 2.0. It works like a viewstate but more powerful, in the sense that the control state cannot be disabled by developers. So even if developers use custom controls and disable the viewstate, the control state remains alive.

Q46. ★What is the purpose of the MustInherit keyword in VB.NET?
A46. The MustInherit keyword in VB.NET is used to create an abstract class.

Q47. ★What does the keyword virtual in C# mean?
A47. The virtual keyword signifies that the methods and properties may be overridden.

Q48. ★How to create a new unique ID for a control?
A48. ControlName.ID = "ControlName" + Guid.NewGuid().ToString();

Q49. ★What is a CLR Stored Procedure?
A49. The CLR Stored Procedures were introduced with SQL Server 2005. They allow writing of stored procedures, triggers, functions, user defined types using .NET languages such as VB.NET and C#.

Q50. ★What is FarPoint?
A50. FarPoint is a third party component that works like an Excel spreadsheet in a web-based environment. It is a product of GrapeCity. Check out http://www.fpoint.com

Q51. ★What are Rad Controls?
A51. Rad controls are third party components that can be used in .NET applications. Rad controls are a product of Telerik. There are Rad controls for ASP.NET, Silverlight, Reporting and Winforms.

Q52. ★Name a few popular open source Content Management Systems based on .NET?
A52. Dotnetnuke, Rainbow, Telerik Sitefinity, Umbraco, Mojo Portal, Kentico CMS

Q53. ★Name a few popular open source E Commerce portals based on .NET?
A53. Nopcommerce, .NETCommerce, Aspdotnetstorefront, dashCommerce

Q54. ★★Which is one of the fastest ADO.NET objects used to fetch data from a backend?
A54. The SqlDataReader object.

Q55. ★★How can you edit data in a repeater control?
A55. It is not possible through a web user interface. A repeater simply pulls and displays data from the backend.

Q56. ★★★What is SetWow and Set64?
A56. To run a 32 bit compiled application on a 65 bit server, you can run the following command on the 64 bit server, on the .NET command prompt:

C:\WINDOWS\Microsoft.NET\Framework64\v2.0.50727\Ldr64.exe SetWow

To set it back to use the 64 bit CLR, run the following command:

C:\WINDOWS\Microsoft.NET\Framework64\v2.0.50727\Ldr64.exe Set64

Q57. ★Which method is used to save data in a dataset?
A57. The AcceptChanges method commits all the changes.

Q58. ★What are partial classes?
A58. A class definition may be split into multiple physical files and still allow a seamless compilation of the classes by the compiler using a partial class. During compile time, the compiler groups all the classes that have the same name, and treats them as a single class.

Q59. ★What is In Proc?
A59. In Proc is a session storage mechanism where in the session state is stored in the memory space of the Aspnet_wp.exe process. In this mechanism, the session state information is lost when IIS reboots.

Q60. ★What is Out Proc?
A60. Out proc is a session storage mechanism where in the session state is stored outside the aspnet_wp.exe. It may be stored in the SQL Server or the State Server(in the aspnet_state.exe process). The Out proc mechanism is used for maintaining sessions across web farms.

Q61. ★★Can a method in C# be created without a name? If yes, how?
A61. Yes, this is possible using **anonymous methods**. These methods are not directly declared; rather they are hooked up to events on the fly.

Example (C#):

```
btnSubmit.Click +=
delegate
{
          MessageBox.Show("dotnetuncle makes it easy");
};
Controls.Add(btnSubmit);
```

Q62. ★★What is the MVP Pattern?
A63. MVC stands for Model-View-Presenter. This pattern allows splitting the application architecture into three roles. The View is usually an interface that is implemented by an ASP.net web page; the Model is the business object. The Presenter negotiates the transfer of data between the other two objects.

Q63. ★★How to set a port for the asp.net development server?
A62. Carry out the following steps:

- ✓ Right click the Project in the Solution Explorer, and then select "Properties"
- ✓ Click "Web" tab.
- ✓ Check "Specific port" instead of "Auto-assign Port".

Q64. ★★Which server side control manages all the web parts in an ASP.NET web page?
A64. WebPartManager

Q65. ★★What is the XPathNavigator class used for?
A65. The XPathNavigator class is used to navigate an XML document that is created using an **XPathDocument** object. The XPathDocument object comprehends the DOM structure of the XML file, and the XPathNavigator object understands the XPath expressions.

Q66. ★Can a structure in C# be overloaded?
A66. Yes.

Q67. ★★★How can you directly call unmanaged code in C#?
A67. You may directly call a function exported from a DLL. For this, declare the method with the **static** and **extern** keywords. Further, attach the **DllImport** attribute to the method.

Q68. ★How do you step through each line of code while debugging?
A68. Use the Step In feature.

Q69. ★★What is the difference between Option Strict On and Option Strict Off in VB.NET?
A69. The Option Strict option allows VB.NET from automatically converting the type of a variable. It is Off by default. If it is On, then automatic conversion does not take place.

Q70. ★Can a GroupBox control contain multiple controls?
A70. Yes it can. Even the Panel and TabPage controls can contain multiple controls inside them.

Q71. ★PictureBox does not have a TabIndex property. True or False?
A71. True

Q72. ★What is the default access specifier for a variable?
A72. Public

Q73. ★Which class can be used to create dynamic creation of types at runtime?

A73. System.Reflection

Q74. ★Can an assembly have a version number?
A74. Yes

Q75. ★What is the lower bound value for an array in C# and VB.NET?
A75. 0

Q76. ★★What is a smart client?
A76. A Smart Client is an application that makes use of the local processing power of a client system, uses XML based web services and may be deployed and updated from a centralized location. Common example of such applications is an Antivirus application installed on your desktop.

Q77. ★★★Which encoding formats are used in Remoting? When to use each of these?
A77. Read on:

✓ **Binary Encoding** – use this when performance of the application is a critical point in the application design
✓ **XML Encoding** – Use this when interoperability with external systems is a key requirement

Q78. ★★What are the two types of objects used in remoting?
A78. The following are the types of objects used in remoting:

Client Activated Objects – these objects are under the control of a lease based lifetime manager that makes sure that the object is collected by the garbage collector when its lifetime completes.

Server Activated Objects – these objects are controlled by the server. They are either "Single Call" or "Singletons". Their lifetime is also controlled by the lease based lifetime model.

Q79. ★★How can we make sure an object can be serialized?
A79. This can be made sure by two ways:

✓ Use a Serializable attribute with the class
✓ Use the ISerializable attribute with the interface

Q80. ★Can a class have more than one base class?
A80. No

Q81. ★How do structures support inheritance?
A81. Structures don't support inheritance.

Q82. ★★★How can we prevent a browser to cache an .ASPX page?
A82. Use the SetNoStore() method as follows, in the ASPX page:

```
<%@ Page Language="C#" %>
<%
    Response.Cache.SetNoStore();
```

```
Response.Write (DateTime.Now.ToLongTimeString ());
%>
```

Q83. ★Is it possible to debug a windows service?
A83. Yes

Q84. ★★What is the max size of a cookie?
A84. The max size of a cookie is 4096 bytes. Also note that not more than 20 cookies per website can be stored on a system.

Q85. ★★What is RootDSE?
A85. The rootDSE is a part of the Lightweight Directory Access Protocol (LDAP 3.0). It is defined as the root of the directory data tree on a directory server. It is not part of any namespace. The purpose of the rootDSE is to provide data about the directory server. Its properties are generally used to query the local active directory.

Q86. ★Is it possible to automate tests in VSTS?
A86. Yes, it is possible to automate tests in VSTS.

Q87. ★What is the Microsoft Web Application Stress tool?
A87. It is a tool used to test the performance of a website. It allows simulating load on a web server.

Q88. ★What is Hungarian notation?
A88. It is the trend of prefixing variables or objects with a few letters (normally three letters) to signify the type of variable or object being declared. For example, a textbox for capturing the 'City' information is generally defined as txtCity.

Q89. ★★What is the use of the DataKeyNames property of a GridView?
A89. The DataKeyNames property is used to get and set the primary key values of the items displayed in a GridView control.

Q90. ★★Can the contents of an uploaded file be read and searched?
A90. Yes, this is possible using Windows Index Search.

Q91. ★★How to restart a Windows Search service?
A91. Go to the run window and type "services.msc". It may ask for an administrator's password, enter that if required. Under Name, double click Windows Search. Now find the Windows Search Properties dialog box. Click Stop and then Start. Lastly, click OK.

Q92. ★★What is delay signing of an assembly?
A92. In case only the public key is required during development time, the delay signing concept may be used. For this, the delay signing attribute in the assemblyinfo.vb or assemblyinfo.cs file has to be set to 'true'.

Q93. ★What is JQuery?

A93. JQuery is a cross-browser javascript library comprised of several reusable methods, designed to simplify client-side scripting. It is a free, open source library having a dual license – one under the MIT licensing agreement, and two under the GNU licensing agreement. It may be downloaded from www.jquery.com.

Q94. ★★★What are the differences between BasicHttpBinding and WsHttpBinding?

A94. The following are the differences:

- ✓ BasicHttpBinding supports old asmx style i.e. the basic WSBindingProfile, where as WsHttpBinding exposes web services using WS-* specification.
- ✓ BasicHttpBinding is generally used for clients that do not have .NET 3.0 installed, whereas WsHttpBinding is used for versions of applications built on .NET 3.0 onwards
- ✓ BasicHttpBinding is based on SOAP 1.1 whereas WsHttpBinding is based on SOAP 1.2 along with WS- addressing specification
- ✓ Former has no default security, whereas later has a default WS-security

Q95. ★★★What is NetTcpBinding?

A95. This is a type of binding in WCF wherein data is sent as binary-encoded SOAP. It consists of support for reliable message transfer, transactions, and security, on top of TCP. It has a disadvantage that both the server and the client have to be built on .NET platform.

Q96. ★What do we use a satellite assembly for?

A96. A satellite assembly is used for containing resource files that correspond to a particular locale. A locale is comprised of Culture and Language. These assemblies are used to deploy applications for multiple geographic locations.

Q97. ★★What is a CompositeControl in .NET?

A97. A CompositeControl is an abstract class in .NET that is inherited by those web controls that have child controls inside them.

Q98. ★★What is the use of the @OutputCache directive in ASP.NET?

A98. This directive is used to declaratively control the caching policies of an aspx web page. The general syntax of this directive is as below:

```
<%@ OutputCache Duration="#ofseconds" Location="Any | Client | Downstream | Server | None"
Shared="True | False" VaryByControl="controlname" VaryByCustom="browser | customstring"
VaryByHeader="headers" VaryByParam="parametername" %>
```

Q99. ★What is the difference between get and post?

A99. A get request is sent using a URL, whereas a post request is sent to the server via the body of the web page. That means a get request can be seen whereas a post cant be seen.

Also note that there isn't any maximum limit on the length of a post request, whereas a get request has a limitation of around 255 characters (though this may vary based on the browser).

A get request is better in terms of performance when compared to a post request.

Q100. What is the difference between Themes and CSS?
A100. Read on:

- ✓ Themes are control based, CSS are HTML based
- ✓ Themes are processed on the server side, CSS is processed at the client side

About the Author

Vishal K. Khanna is a developer, an IT manager and an author. He is the owner and author of www.dotnetuncle.com, a .NET FAQ website.

Vishal K. Khanna was born in Manila, Philippines, on 1st September 1978, and grew up in South Delhi, India. He did his early schooling at Elizabeth Seton School in Manila and later moved to India. He completed his senior secondary schooling from SBDAV Public School, New Delhi and then moved on to Bangalore where he pursued his B.Sc. in Computer Science from Garden City College *(GCC)*, and Masters in Computer Applications *(MCA)* from Dayananda Sagar College of Management & Information Technology *(DSCMIT)*. He holds certifications from Microsoft, PMI.org and Salesforce.com. Vishal has worked in multiple IT companies and is experienced in architecting enterprise class web applications on a variety of technical platforms and domains.

He likes spending good time with his family. Besides that, he has a great passion for writing and participating in technical forums. Vishal also enjoys partying with friends and travelling to unexplored destinations.

www.ingramcontent.com/pod-product-compliance
Lightning Source LLC
Chambersburg PA
CBHW071205050326
40689CB00011B/2247